W9-ARQ-380

Sourdough

BAKING

*Fabulous recipes for bread machines
and traditional methods.*

Susan Draudt

er™

FISHER
BOOKS

Publishers: Bill Fisher
Howard Fisher
Helen V. Fisher
J. McCrary

Editor: Helen V. Fisher

**Cover design
and illustraton:**   David Fischer

Book design: David Fischer &
Edgar H. Allard

Illustrations: David Fischer

**Library of Congress
Cataloging-in-Publication Data**

Draudt, Susan Brown.
   Sourdough baking : fabulous
recipes for bread machines and
traditional methods /
Susan Draudt.
     p.   cm
   Includes index.
   ISBN 1-55561-067-6: $9.95
   1. Cookery (Sourdough)
   I. Title.
   TX770.S66D73   1994
   641.8'15—dc20   94-34432

Published by Fisher Books
4239 W. Ina Road, Suite #101
Tucson, AZ 85741
(602) 744-6110

© 1994 by Fisher Books
Printed in USA
Printing 10 9 8 7 6 5 4 3 2

All rights reserved. No part of this book may be reproduced or transmitted in any form or by any means, electronic or mechanical, including photocopy, recording or any information storage or retrieval system, without written permission from the publisher, except by a reviewer who may quote brief passages.

Notice: The information in this book is true and complete to the best of our knowledge. It is offered with no guarantees on the part of the author or Fisher Books. The author and publisher disclaim all liability in connection with use of this book. Fisher Books are available at special quantity discounts for educational use. Special books or book excerpts can also be created to fit specific needs. For details please write or telephone.

Contents

About the Author

The love of preparing food and presenting a beautiful, delicious dish was the beginning of Susan Draudt's career in foods.

Upon graduation from the University of California at Los Angeles, with a degree in Home Economics, Susan quickly embarked on a multi-faceted career. She supplied consumer information for a large grocery chain, plus recipe development and food styling.

She also shares her talents and experience as an enthusiastic teacher at cooking schools, department stores and cookware shops.

Susan enjoys working with various kitchen appliances and has acted as instructor for different manufacturer's demonstration teams. She has also authored *Food Processor Cookery, 30-Minute Meals, Microwaving for 1 or 2*, and *Microwaving with an International Flair*.

Bread baking has always been one of her favorite activities. So, it was a natural step to develop recipes using both traditional methods as well as bread machines.

Most of her work has been in California. However, Susan, husband Dennis and children Danielle and Michael lived in Massachusetts for several years. The exposure to the East has given her a new appreciation for regional flavors.

At present the family resides in a Los Angeles suburb. Susan does food styling for various food companies and equipment manufacturers across the country.

Introduction

Sourdough Baking

The aroma of baking bread is one of the best fragrances that can be created in a home. This old-fashioned activity is becoming a welcome pastime in this modern age. There is something very satisfying about making your own daily bread. New techniques join with traditional methods and offer you choices not available before.

Here are wonderful ways to personalize the most basic food—bread. Making and shaping breads can also be a rewarding social event. Strong hands make kneading a simple task, we've even had competitions as to which bread looked and tasted the best. Get friends and family involved and reap the benefits of deliciously different breads.

Leavening bread with bits of "soured" dough saved from the last batch has been a baker's secret since the early Egyptians. The special flavor and texture that this "soured" dough gave the bread was not appreciated and cultivated in America until the mid 1800s when the California gold miners began to consider their "starter" as a coveted commodity. Word of the wonderful bread being baked in the gold rush country spread as fast as the gold mining fever did, and San Francisco quickly became the sourdough capital of the world.

The quest for gold moved north to Alaska and sourdough moved with it. We now have a rivalry between Alaskan and San Franciscan sourdough. Prospectors were even known to drink the fermented liquid that forms on the top of the starter. It was called *hooch* and it brought some warmth and comfort to the prospectors during cold winter nights while they looked for the elusive gold.

Sourdough flavor and texture is easy to incorporate into most any type of bread recipe. Classic sourdough, French bread, pancakes, waffles, pizza dough and even cornbread benefit when you use a starter in the recipe.

There are several ingredients that you can use to make starters. Flour and water are the traditional ingredients for sourdough starters. Try a yogurt-based starter for an extra tangy flavor. The beer-based starter is great with a whole-wheat cheese bread. There are recipes for six different starters. Feel free to try any starter in any recipe. The *proportions* of liquid to flour are all the same in each starter recipe.

Creating your own starter to use for sourdough baking is easy. If you are a purist, you can create your starter with just flour and water and let it set out to catch yeast spores from the air. This takes some time and you're never quite sure what flavor you will end up with. Equal parts of flour and liquid are the basic ingredients, with the addition of a small amount of yeast, potato, yogurt or even an aspen twig to begin the fermentation process. By adding a small amount of active dry yeast when you first make your starter you guarantee the success and flavor of your starter. After a period of about 24 hours the starter will begin to bubble and ferment. The starter now is ready to be used in your baking.

There is real joy and satisfaction in sourdough baking when you create your own starter and keep it alive to use again and again in different recipes. This ancient method is as old as the art of baking itself. By following this method you keep alive the art and history of baking by introducing your own personal variations to basic recipes.

Recipes in this book use yeast in addition to the starter. By using both, the time required to produce loaves of delicious bread is shorter than by using starter alone. The recipes in this collection can be used for traditional baking methods as well as for bread-machine baking as long you make sure the proportions are correct for use in the bread machine.

Bread texture will be improved if you use bread flour because it has a higher gluten content. All-purpose flour (bleached or unbleached) can be substituted for bread flour.

If you want to use different types of flour made from other grains like rye or buckwheat in a bread recipe, always be sure to use at least 50% wheat flour to get the best texture and volume.

Water and milk can be used interchangeably with very little change to the bread. Yeast is used to assist in the rising of the dough. One 1/4-oz. packet of active dry yeast (2-1/2 teaspoons) is enough to raise 2 loaves of bread dough in which approximately 7 cups of flour have been used. The same amount of yeast can also be used in a single loaf recipe if desired.

When the dough has satisfactorily risen it can be shaped into a variety of shapes. This is usually done after the first rising. If you want to glaze the top of the loaf, do it just before baking so the glaze doesn't inhibit the rise.

The Components of Bread Baking

Flour: Wheat flour, with its high gluten content, forms the structure for most breads. Flours such as rye and buckwheat or flours made from other grains can be used, but should be combined with at least 50% wheat flour to help the dough to rise nicely.

Sugars: Small amounts of white sugar, brown sugar, honey or molasses are used to feed the yeast. The sugar also adds a sweet flavor, tenderizes the texture, and helps to brown the crust.

Fats: Oils, butter or margarine. Fat is not always necessary in bread baking, but it helps to tenderize the product and adds a richer flavor.

Liquids: Milk or water are most commonly used for bread baking; however any liquid will work. The liquid binds all the ingredients together and allows the gluten to form during kneading. The proportion of liquid to flour directly affects the texture and rising ability of the bread. Milk gives the bread a softer texture; water gives a slightly coarser texture. For a different flavor try substituting orange juice or buttermilk (in equivalent amounts) for milk or water.

Salt: The obvious reason for salt is for taste, but it also helps to control the rise. Too much salt will slow down the action of the yeast; not enough salt will weaken the gluten structure.

Sourdough Starter: Sourdough starter is used for leavening breads and doughs. It also gives a tangy "sour" flavor and slightly denser texture.

Sponge: The classic method for making sourdough uses a *sponge.* A sponge consists of sourdough starter, liquid and usually one-half the flour. The ingredients are mixed together, covered and set aside to ferment.

Making "classic sourdough" bread takes much longer because the sponge needs 2 to 24 hours to ferment. At the end of this time the sponge should be full of bubbles. Each rising will also take from 2 to 4 hours. To ensure a good rise, the dough should be placed in an 80F (25C) environment. The rise will require more time in a cooler temperature. Then bake as directed in the recipe.

This is a very time-consuming method but the taste and texture results make it all worthwhile. Any bread recipe can be made using the sponge technique.

The sponge is not always necessary in sourdough baking if yeast is added to the recipe, as in the recipes in this book. The sponge method does provide added sour flavor and better texture. Yeast increases the leavening properties of the starter.

Eggs: The addition of an egg or two gives bread products a lighter texture and a lovely light-yellow tint.

Types of Flour and Grains: Many markets carry a wide variety of flours and types of grains for making bread. Health-food and specialty stores also have a wonderful assortment to choose from.

Amaranth: This high-protein grain was a staple in the Aztec diet. It is available as flour and as as whole grain.

Barley: A slightly sweet, mild-flavored grain. Due to its low gluten content, it should always be used with wheat flour for bread baking.

Brown Rice: Because rice flour has no gluten it is recommended only for pastry making.

Buckwheat: This strong-flavored flour is often used for pancakes. Because buckwheat has a low gluten content it is often combined with wheat flour. Buckwheat flour is light brown with dark specks.

Corn: Corn is dried and ground into a coarse meal. Corn flour, a finer grind, is also known as *masa harina.* Corn grows in yellow, white and blue varieties and can be used interchangeably.

Gluten Flour: Gluten is the substance that remains when high-protein hard spring wheat is washed to remove most of the starch. Gluten flour can be added to improve the texture of bread made with all-purpose flour or flour with a low gluten content.

Graham Flour: A soft whole-wheat flour used for "Graham Crackers" or any baking that does not require a high gluten flour.

Millet: Used in its whole form, this small yellow grain is added to breads to give a nutty texture.

Mesquite Flour: A fine-textured, tan-colored flour made from dried pods of the mesquite tree. Mesquite flour was a staple in the diet of Southwestern native peoples.

Oats: Oats are available in several forms: flour, bran, berries and flakes. The most common form is the one we eat for breakfast. These oat grains have been steamed and flattened into flakes to speed up the cooking time. To make your own oat flour grind the flakes in a food processor. Oat flour is low in gluten so use 1/3 oat flour to 2/3 wheat flour for yeast breads.

Quinoa: A new-ancient grain originally from South America. It is similar in appearance to millet and can be used the same way.

Rye: A hearty grain that has long been associated with European breads such as rye and pumpernickel. Flour ground from the whole rye berry is often called *pumpernickel flour.* Rye flour is low in gluten content. Used in a yeast bread by itself, rye flour produces a very dense loaf.

Semolina: Made from durum wheat which is very high in protein and gluten. It is usually used to make pasta, but also makes wonderful light yellow bread. Semolina has a semi-coarse grind.

Spelt: An ancient wheat that contains more protein than wheat. Spelt has a nutty flavor and can be used as a substitute for wheat flour.

Triticale: A new hybrid grain that is as nutritious as wheat and tastes slightly like rye. Triticale has less gluten content than wheat but can be used successfully in bread recipes.

Wheat: The grain of any cereal grass of the genus *Truticum.* The high gluten content of wheat has made it the mainstay of bread baking for the whole world.

All-Purpose Flour: A multipurpose flour made from a combination of soft and hard wheat. It can be used for bread as well as pastries.

Bread Flour: Flour milled from hard red spring wheat. Its high gluten content makes it good for yeast bread baking.

Cracked Wheat: Whole-wheat kernels which are coarsely ground are called cracked. When used in bread, cracked wheat gives a nice crunchy texture.

Whole-Wheat Flour: A coarse textured flour made from the whole-wheat kernel.

Wheat Berries: This is the whole kernel of wheat. They are very hard and should be soaked overnight before using.

Wheat Bran: The partially ground husk of wheat often separated from flour meal by sifting. Bran is frequently added back to bread for its flavor and texture.

Wheat Germ: The embryo of the wheat kernel that has a nutty flavor. It is sold toasted or raw and should be refrigerated to prevent it from becoming rancid.

Yeast: When you purchase yeast, the package or container will have an expiration date on it. It should be stored in an airtight container in the refrigerator or freezer. Because yeast is a living organism, it loses its power as it ages. For best results all yeast should be used before the expiration date. Yeast can be frozen for longer storage.

When yeast is used in recipes (in addition to starter), it should first be *proofed.* Proofing tests the yeast to make certain it is active. As a reminder, this is usually the first instruction in a recipe. Yeast is proofed by adding it to warm liquid (110F or 45C) and sugar. Stir to dissolve the yeast and let it stand 10 minutes. The mixture should swell and foam, *proof* that the yeast is active. If yeast is old and does not swell, discard it as it will not work as required.

Active dry yeast: Dry granules of a living micro-organism that come to life by the addition of warm liquid, about 110F (45C). Activated yeast gives off carbon-dioxide bubbles that cause the dough to rise. One 1/4-oz. packet of active dry yeast is equal to 2-1/2 teaspoons of dry yeast.

Compressed cake yeast: A soft moist form of yeast with each cube having the leavening ability of one packet of active dry yeast. It is foil-wrapped and can be found in the dairy/deli case in the grocery store. Moist yeast is highly perishable and should be stored in the refrigerator or freezer and should be used before the expiration date. One .6-oz. cube is equal to 1 packet of active dry yeast.

Rapid-rising yeast: This is sold in the active dry yeast form and will raise dough in half the normal time. It can be used in place of regular active yeast for regular baking and in bread machines.

Rapid-rising yeast: This is sold in the active dry yeast form and will raise dough in half the normal time. It can be used in place of regular active yeast for regular baking and in bread machines.

Mixing and Kneading The Dough

Once you have assembled the ingredients for your recipe and have proofed the yeast following directions on the package or in your recipe, you are ready to mix and knead the dough by one of the following methods.

Hand Method

Use a large mixing bowl so it will be easy to stir the ingredients together. Add the ingredients in the order specified in the recipe. When the dough is completely mixed, place it on a smooth surface that has been lightly sprinkled with flour to keep the dough from sticking. If you are making a rye bread or one that tends to be more sticky, you might want to coat your hands with a little vegetable oil.

To knead the dough properly, place one or both hands into the center of the ball of dough and push it down and away from you. Fold the far edge of the dough over, bringing it towards you. Rotate dough a quarter turn and then repeat. Depending on the type of bread you are making, the kneading process usually takes about 10 minutes.

Biscuits and coffeecake doughs usually need less kneading; follow the recipe instructions. When properly kneaded, dough should be soft and smooth. To rise, place the dough in a clean, oiled mixing bowl. Turn the dough over in the bowl so all sides are lightly covered with oil. Cover it loosely with a towel or plastic wrap to keep it moist and place it in a draft-free warm (80F or 25C) area to rise.

Bread-Machine Method

Bread machines are very popular and make one loaf at a time. A 1-pound loaf requires about 2 cups of flour, a

1-1/2-pound loaf of bread about 3 cups of flour. Carefully measuring ingredients is the key to a perfect loaf of bread.

The bread machine mixes, kneads, rises and bakes the dough automatically. Follow the instruction book that comes with your machine and add all the ingredients to the baking pan in the order specified. You can have a great loaf of bread in about 2-1/2 hours. If you wish, set the timer before you retire and wake in the morning to freshly baked bread, ready for the toaster or to be made into French Toast.

Electric Mixer with a Dough Hook Method

Sturdy electric mixers with a dough hook can mix the ingredients to form the dough. The dough hook will also knead the bread. Add the ingredients in the order specified in the recipe. The time for kneading by machine is usually slightly less than by hand. Check your mixer instructions for appropriate kneading time. The dough should form a single large ball. If the dough is too sticky and doesn't gather into a smooth ball as it is kneaded, add a tablespoon or more flour at a time. If the dough seems too dry, add water, one tablespoon at a time.

Food-Processor Method

Bread dough can be mixed and kneaded very easily in the food processor. Depending on the strength and size of your food processor, you should successfully be able to make 1 or 2 loaves at a time. Kneading in a food processor takes about 60 seconds. Use the bread-kneading blade that comes with a food processor.

The usual order for making bread is to add the dry ingredients and any shortening, oil, butter or margarine and mix them together. Then with the machine running, slowly pour in liquid ingredients. The dough should gather into a smooth ball. To knead dough, continue running the machine for about 1 minute. Remove the lid to check the consistency of dough. It should be soft and not sticky to your fingers. If dough does not gather into a ball while kneading and it seems too wet, add flour, one tablespoon at a time, while machine is running. If dough is dry and crumbly or stiff, add water, one tablespoon at a time until dough is smooth and not sticky.

Rising

Yeast and sourdough bread doughs need to rise to stretch and strengthen the gluten structure for a firm texture. Carbon dioxide is given off by the yeast and develops bubbles that stretch the dough. Two risings is the norm. For the first rise, the dough should double in size. It is then punched down to get rid of any large air bubbles and shaped for baking.

Some breads call for a single rising which gives a crumbly texture. If you don't have time to shape the dough after its first rising, it can be punched down and left to rise again before being shaped and placed in the baking pan for its final rising before baking. Bread dough can also rise in the refrigerator overnight, or be wrapped and frozen for future use. Before using refrigerated or frozen dough, let dough come to room temperature.

Shaping and Baking

The dough is usually shaped for baking after the first rising. If the dough seems to resist when shaping, let it rest for about 10 minutes before shaping it. After the dough has risen it can be shaped into a variety of shapes, such as loaves, braids or rolls. Some suggestions here and on the next page will help to spark your imagination.

If you want to glaze the top of the loaf, do it just before baking so it doesn't inhibit the rise.

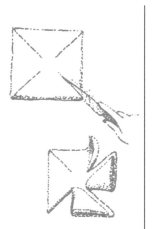

A pinwheel shape can be used for a loaf or for rolls.

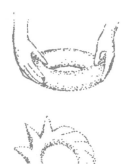

A snipped ring creates a decorative edge.

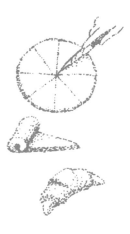

Preparing crescent rolls.

Classic Bread Shapes

Braid

Leaf

Ring

Pinwheel

Round

Coil

Pull-apart

Bowl-shaped

Baguette

Net-covered

Star

Twist

Roll Shapes

Crescent

Knot

Cloverleaf

French

Sticks

Parker House

Hot Dog &
Burger

Round,
seeded edge

Baked Results of Various Pan Shapes

Cake Pan

Tube Pan

Bundt Pan

Muffin Pan

Spring Pan

Crust Glazes

Shiny Crust

1. For a dark golden-brown top, brush unbaked loaves with a mixture of 1 egg and 2 tablespoons water just before baking.
2. For a shiny clear top, brush unbaked dough with a mixture of 1 egg white and 1 tablespoon water just before baking.
3. Either of these glazes work well to secure seeds on top of bread. Brush on glaze then sprinkle liberally with seeds before baking.
4. If an even shinier crust is desired, rebrush top of bread about 15 minutes before removing from oven.

Crisp Crust

1. Place a pan of hot water on bottom rack of oven.
2. Spray baking bread with fine mist of water 2 or 3 times during the first 5 minutes of baking.
3. When bread is baked remove from pan and place in oven for 10 more minutes.

Soft Crust

1. Brush with melted butter, margarine or milk as soon as bread is removed from oven.
2. For a soft sweet crust, brush just-baked loaves with honey, molasses, maple syrup or corn syrup diluted 50-50 with water.

Chewy European Crust

Mix 1 teaspoon cornstarch with 3/4 cup water. Bring to a boil (easy to do in a microwave oven). Stir until cool. Brush on unbaked dough.

Slashing

The practice of slashing the tops of bread loaves may have originated with the early community ovens in Europe. Each household prepared their own dough, then cut its identifying mark in the top because it was baked in a community oven.

Today, making slash marks on the tops of loaves gives distinction to each loaf, helps to release steam, and helps the rise. Free-form breads and baguettes are usually the ones marked. Use a sharp knife or razor blade as the professional bakers do, cutting 1/16 or 1/8 inch deep. Do not cut deeper or you may deflate the loaf.

Baking Equipment

Breads can be baked in an infinite assortment of shapes or pans. The shape and size of the loaf will determine the baking time.

Traditional: Loaf shapes are great for slicing and fit readily in the toaster. A 9" x 5" pan accommodates a recipe made with 5 to 6 cups flour while 8" x 4" pans make 2 loaves from a 5- to 6-cup flour recipe. Mini loaf pans should be filled only half full with dough.

Bread Sheet: Used to bake hand-shaped or free-form loaves. Sheet should be at least twice the width of the dough. If the surface is not non-stick, spray it with non-stick coating, grease it or sprinkle with cornmeal.

Baking Equipment

Baking pans

Baking sheet

Baguette pan

Baking stone

Non-traditional baking containers

Cloche

Banneton

Springform pan

Baguette Pans: These look like wavy baking sheets with 2 to 4 long narrow furrows. The dough is placed into the furrows that give the bread the classical French or Italian shape. These pans are also available with thinner furrows to bake crispy breadsticks.

Bread-baking Stones: Although they are called *stones*, most are made from a porous ceramic material. The stone absorbs moisture from the dough as it bakes to give it a crisp crust. Place the stone in the oven, then preheat the oven for 30 minutes. The shaped bread dough is placed directly on the stone to bake.

Non-traditional Baking Containers: Bread can be baked in coffee cans, new terracotta flower pots, pie plates, spring-form pans, frying pans, casserole dishes or muffin tins. Use your imagination.

Banneton: French bakers rise the dough in these baskets. Some baskets are lined with linen. The distinctive design of the basket leaves its imprint on the dough. The risen dough is inverted onto a baking sheet for baking. The basket is removed and the baking sheet and bread are placed in the oven to bake.

Baking Cloche: Cloche in French means *hat*. A cloche is an unglazed ceramic baking pan with a dome-shaped top. The lid is soaked in water before baking. The lid covers the baking dish and gives off steam during the baking to produce a nice crispy-crusted loaf.

Instant-Read Thermometer: This small thermometer usually has a range up to 220F (105C). Its long spike is placed in liquid to measure the temperature before yeast is added. For best results, the temperature of the liquid should be 110F (45C).

Bread Knife: A knife with a long serrated or scalloped edge blade which cuts bread nicely when you use a gentle sawing action. Electric knives also work very well for slicing bread.

Storage of Bread

Bread placed in a plastic bag or wrapped in plastic wrap or foil should keep at room temperature for 2 to 3 days. Refrigerated wrapped bread will last about one week. Frozen bread, well wrapped, will be tasty for about 6 months.

High-Altitude Baking

The changes in bread baking at altitudes above 3,000 feet are minimal. The flour may be drier and absorb slightly more liquid. Most recipes in this book suggest adding the flour a little at a time until you get a soft pliable dough. At higher altitudes the rising time may be slightly less than suggested in the recipe. Just remember the dough should be doubled in size after each rising to be ready. Increasing the baking temperature 25F (15C) also helps to give good results.

Tasty Additions to the Basic Bread Recipe

You can create your own favorite bread recipes by adding any combination of these ingredients. I suggest adding up to 1 cup per loaf of any combination of ingredients. For best results be sure to chop any large ingredients to about the size of a raisin.

Savory	Sweet
Bell pepper	Granola cereal
Green onions	Raisins
Shredded carrots	Currants
Shredded zucchini	Dried fruit
Dried tomatoes	Shredded apple
Shredded cheese	Dried cherries
Chopped nuts	Dried blueberries
Wheat germ	Dried cranberries
Sprouted seeds	Dried strawberries
Garlic, minced	Chocolate chips
Fresh herbs	Shredded coconut
Sunflower seeds	Chopped dates
Caraway seeds	Chopped nuts
Green chiles	Prunes

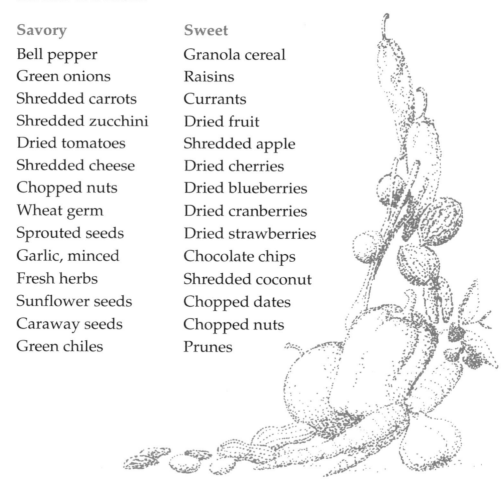

Tips

General Tips

- If you buy large quantities of flour that will not be used within six months, wrap it tightly and keep it in the freezer until needed.
- To measure flour accurately, stir it, then gently spoon it into a dry measuring cup. Level the top with the straight edge of a spatula or knife.
- If you want to grind your own grain, 1 cup of most grains yields 1-1/4 cups flour. 1 cup of ground rolled oats yields 7/8 cup of flour.
- Use a thermometer to check the temperature of liquids before adding yeast. Temperature more than 110F (45C) will kill the yeast.
- If your kitchen is cool and you need a warm spot for dough to rise in, heat your oven on the lowest setting for 10 minutes, then turn it off. Place the covered dough in the oven with the oven light turned on.
- For a soft crust, spread the crust with butter or margarine as soon as it comes from the oven.
- For a shiny crust, brush the top of the bread dough (before baking) with a mixture of 1 egg and 1 tablespoon of water whipped together.
- Allow the bread to cool completely before slicing. An electric knife slices very neatly.
- Slashing the top of the bread dough lets the steam escape and gives an attractive appearance.
- The higher the sugar content of the bread the more quickly it browns.
- If your bread starts to brown too fast or too much in one spot, cover the loaf or spot with foil.
- For a change try a different starter such as the rye- or beer-based starter instead of your usual one.

- If the sourdough flavor is too strong, stir 1/2 teaspoon baking soda into the flour and starter mixture.
- If the tap water in your area has a very strong taste I recommend using bottled or purified water.
- One loaf (3 - 4 cups flour) of bread dough will make about 12 rolls.

Tips on Ingredients

- To give a firmer texture to your bread add 2 to 3 tablespoons of cornmeal to the dough for each loaf.
- To leaven your bread using only sourdough starter, mix the correct amount of starter with 2 cups of the flour and 1-1/2 cups of the liquid. Mix all together. Cover loosely and set in a warm (80F or 25C) spot for about 8 hours or overnight, until mixture is full of bubbles. Continue with recipe as usual. Rising times will be about 2 to 3 hours, so check rising volume carefully. Bake as directed.
- Bread enhancers are a mixture of citric acid, malt and gluten used originally by professional chefs to give more volume and a better texture to their breads. They are available for the home baker. About 1 tablespoon per loaf is usually added. These are often recommended for bread machines.
- If you choose to weigh your flour, 1 cup of all-purpose or bread flour equals 4 oz., 4 cups of flour equals 1 lb. A 5-lb. package of flour yields 20 cups. However, 1 cup of whole-wheat flour equals 4-1/2 oz.; 3-1/2 cups of whole-wheat flour equals 1 lb.

Tips for Baking

- When using a glass baking pan, lower the oven temperature by 25F (5C).
- To use your sourdough starter in a "non-sourdough" recipe, for one cup of sourdough starter added decrease liquid by 2/3 cup and flour by 1/3 cup. Do not alter the amount of yeast if there is any in the recipe.

Tips on Leftover Bread

- Try these ideas for leftover bread: bread pudding, strata, individual pizzas, French toast , croutons for salads or soups, stuffing for turkey, chicken, pork chops or seafood.
- Use leftover bread to make bread crumbs. Grind leftovers in a food processor or blender, freeze extras.

Tips on Mixing Dough

- Bread flour with its higher gluten content tends to absorb more liquid than all-purpose flour. If you use all-purpose flour in a recipe calling for bread flour, start by using slightly less water and add as needed.

Tips on Rising Dough

- To check dough to see if it has doubled in volume for its first rising, push your knuckle about 1/2 inch into the dough. If the dent remains, the dough has risen enough.
- For the second rising, after the dough has been shaped, use time and appearance to gauge when it is ready for baking.
- After kneading the dough let it rest about 10 minutes to relax. It will be easier to shape.

Tips on Toasting Nuts

Toasting nuts is not necessary, but toasting gives them a much richer flavor. There are two easy methods.
- Baking method: Spread nuts in a single layer on a baking sheet. Place in a 350F (175C) oven for about 10 minutes. You will be able to tell when they are done by the wonderful aroma. Do not let them burn.
- Frying-pan method: place nuts in a frying pan over medium heat. Stir constantly to brown on all sides. Depending on size of nuts they should take 5 to 10 minutes.

Traditional Baking

Sourdough Starter Basics

Multi- and Single-Grain Breads

Fruit and Nut Breads

Savory Breads

Popovers, Pancakes and Waffles

Main Course Breads

Sourdough Starter Basics

Starters act as leavening agents as well as lending a wonderful sour flavor and chewy texture to any baked product. All the starter recipes in this book are made with the same flour-to-liquid proportions so they are interchangeable in any recipe. Try recipes using the different starters. You will find an amazing variance in flavor.

An additional small amount of active dry yeast has been included in each bread recipe to guarantee an even quality for all breads and to speed up the preparation time. If you prefer not to use added yeast, follow the sponge method on page 6.

Starter preparation basics.

1. Mix starters in glass or plastic containers that can hold 3 times the amount of ingredients. Starter expands as it ferments.
2. Metal spoons and containers are not recommended for use as they might give an undesirable flavor.
3. Cover containers loosely to let fresh air in and keep unwanted flavors out.
4. Store at about 80F (25C) for 3 to 5 days until mixture begins to bubble. Stir 3 or 4 times a day.
5. Once starter is bubbly, refrigerate until ready to use.
6. Starters should be replenished with 1 cup of flour and 1 cup of water for every 1 cup of starter used.
7. If you do not use the starter within 10 days, remove 1 cup of starter and replenish with 1 cup flour and 1 cup water, stir well.
8. A clear liquid will rise to the top of the starter. Just stir it back into the mixture.

9. If the starter turns a strange color (pink to orange) or smells bad, discard it and start over.

Using starter in recipes.*

1. Let starter come to room temperature before using.
2. Measure starter in liquid-type measuring cups.

Replenishing starter to keep it for future use.

1. After removing amount of starter needed for recipe, stir in 1 cup water and 1 cup flour.
2. Stir until mixture is smooth.
3. Cover loosely and refrigerate until needed.
4. Starter should be replenished or "fed" every 7 to 10 days. If this is done, starter can be kept indefinitely.
5. If you don't plan on using your starter for a long period of time, it can be frozen for about 2 months.
6. Defrost starter and let stand out overnight or until it begins to bubble.

* Sourdough Starter is available in dry form in 1/2 oz. packages. Read the package notes to make sure it can be used in bread machines as well as in traditional baking.

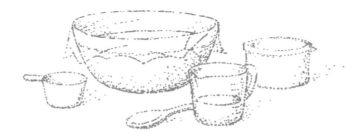

Sourdough Starter

Sourdough starters can be shared with friends and kept or replenished for years. This basic starter blends well in any recipe.

2 cups water

1 teaspoooon active dry yeast

2 cups all-purpose or bread flour

3 tablespoons sugar

In a 2-quart glass or plastic bowl, combine all ingredients. Stir until smooth. Cover loosely so a small amount of fresh air can get in. Place in a warm spot (80F or 25C is perfect) for 3 to 5 days, stirring twice a day. The starter should have bubbles on the surface and begin to smell slightly sour, but still fresh. At this point it is ready to use and should be kept refrigerated. After a few days a small amount of liquid will gather on top, stir it back into the mixture before using.

To replenish or feed the starter after some has been used in a recipe, stir in 1 cup of flour and 1 cup of water. If you have not used any of the starter in a week, remove 1 cup of it and discard, or give it to someone to bake with. Add 1 cup of water and 1 cup of flour and stir until smooth. This process can be kept up indefinitely. If mold should form on the top, skim it off and stir well. If the starter turns pink, orange or any other strange color, throw it out and begin a new batch.

Yogurt Starter

When you are in a hurry, this starter gives an extra-tangy flavor that develops quickly.

1/2 cup nonfat milk

1-1/2 cups plain yogurt

2 cups all-purpose or bread flour

1 teaspoon active dry yeast

In a 2-quart glass or plastic bowl, combine all ingredients. Stir until smooth. Cover loosely so a small amount of fresh air can get in. Place in a warm spot (80F or 25C is perfect) for 3 to 5 days, stirring twice a day. The starter should have bubbles on the surface and begin to smell slightly sour, but still fresh. At this point it is ready to use and should be kept refrigerated. After a couple of days a small amount of liquid will gather on top, stir it back into the mixture before using.

To replenish or feed the starter after some has been used in a recipe, stir in 1 cup of flour and 1 cup of water. If you have not used any of the starter in a week, remove 1 cup of it and discard, or give it to someone to bake with. Add 1 cup of water and 1 cup of flour and stir until smooth. This process can be kept up indefinitely. If mold should form on the top, skim it off and stir well. If the starter turns pink, orange or any other strange color, throw it out and begin a new batch.

Whole-Wheat Starter

Any recipe with whole-wheat flour will work with this starter.
Or, if you want to add a little texture to a white-flour recipe,
use this starter.

2 cups water

2 cups whole-wheat flour

1 teaspoon active dry yeast

In a 2-quart glass or plastic bowl, combine all ingredients.
Stir until smooth. Cover loosely so a small amount of fresh
air can get in. Place in a warm spot (80F or 25C is perfect)
for 3 to 5 days, stirring twice a day. The starter should have
bubbles on the surface and begin to smell slightly sour, but
still fresh. At this point it is ready to use and should be
kept refrigerated. After a couple of days a small amount of
liquid will gather on top, stir it back into the mixture
before using.

To replenish or feed the starter after some has been used
in a recipe, stir in 1 cup of flour and 1 cup of water. If you
have not used any of the starter in a week, remove 1 cup
of it and discard, or give it to someone to bake with. Add
1 cup of water and 1 cup of flour and stir until smooth.
This process can be kept up indefinitely. If mold should
form on the top, skim it off and stir well. If the starter
turns pink, orange or any other strange color, throw it
out and begin a new batch.

Potato Starter

To get the water for this starter cook 3 large peeled potatoes in water until tender. Save 2 cups water from potatoes and cool to room temperature.

2 cups potato water

2 cups all-purpose or bread flour

1 teaspoon active dry yeast

In a 2-quart glass or plastic bowl, combine all ingredients. Stir until smooth. Cover loosely so a small amount of fresh air can get in. Place in a warm spot (80F or 25C is perfect) for 3 to 5 days, stirring twice a day. The starter should have bubbles on the surface and begin to smell slightly sour, but still fresh. At this point it is ready to use and should be kept refrigerated. After a couple of days a small amount of liquid will gather on top, stir it back into the mixture before using.

To replenish or feed the starter after some has been used in a recipe, stir in 1 cup of flour and 1 cup of water. If you have not used any of the starter in a week, remove 1 cup of it and discard, or give it to someone to bake with. Add 1 cup of water and 1 cup of flour and stir until smooth. This process can be kept up indefinitely. If mold should form on the top, skim it off and stir well. If the starter turns pink, orange or any other strange color, throw it out and begin a new batch.

Beer Starter

Wonderful with cheese breads and whole-wheat-grain breads.

2 cups flat beer

2 cups all-purpose or bread flour

1 teaspoon active dry yeast

In a 2-quart glass or plastic bowl, combine all ingredients. Stir until smooth. Cover loosely so a small amount of fresh air can get in. Place in a warm spot (80F or 25C is perfect) for 3 to 5 days, stirring twice a day. The starter should have bubbles on the surface and begin to smell slightly sour, but still fresh. At this point it is ready to use and should be kept refrigerated. After a couple of days a small amount of liquid will gather on top, stir it back into the mixture before using.

To replenish or feed the starter after some has been used in a recipe, stir in 1 cup of flour and 1 cup of water. If you have not used any of the starter in a week, remove 1 cup of it and discard, or give it to someone to bake with. Add 1 cup of water and 1 cup of flour and stir until smooth. This process can be kept up indefinitely. If mold should form on the top, skim it off and stir well. If the starter turns pink, orange or any other strange color, throw it out and begin a new batch.

Rye Starter

For rye breads of all types or if you just want some rye flavor.

2 cups water

2 cups rye flour

1 teaspoon active dry yeast

In a 2-quart glass or plastic bowl, combine all ingredients. Stir until smooth. Cover loosely so a small amount of fresh air can get in. Place in a warm spot (80F or 25C is perfect) for 3 to 5 days, stirring twice a day. The starter should have bubbles on the surface and begin to smell slightly sour, but still fresh. At this point it is ready to use and should be kept refrigerated. After a couple of days a small amount of liquid will gather on top, stir it back into the mixture before using.

To replenish or feed the starter after some has been used in a recipe, stir in 1 cup of flour and 1 cup of water. If you have not used any of the starter in a week, remove 1 cup of it and discard, or give it to someone to bake with. Add 1 cup of water and 1 cup of flour and stir until smooth. This process can be kept up indefinitely. If mold should form on the top, skim it off and stir well. If the starter turns pink, orange or any other strange color, throw it out and begin a new batch.

Quick French Bread

Place a pan of hot water on the lower rack of your oven before baking. The steam gives a really thick crunchy crust.

1-1/4 cups warm milk, 110F (45C)

2 teaspoons active dry yeast

1 cup sourdough starter

1 tablespoon sugar

1 tablespoon oil

5 to 6 cups bread flour

2 teaspoons salt

1 tablespoon cornmeal

Water

In a large mixing bowl combine the warm milk, yeast, sourdough starter and sugar. Stir and let stand for 10 minutes. Mix in oil, one half the bread flour and salt. Gradually add enough of the remaining bread flour to make a soft dough. Turn dough out onto a lightly floured smooth surface. Clean and grease the mixing bowl, set aside. Knead the dough for about 10 minutes until smooth and elastic. Place dough in greased bowl, turning to coat all sides. Cover and let rise until double in size, about 1 hour. Punch dough down and shape into 2 baguette shapes or 1 large round. Slash the top of each 4 or 5 times with a sharp knife. Place on baking sheet sprinkled with cornmeal. Cover and let rise until double in size, about 1 hour. Preheat oven to 375F (190C). Fill a baking pan with 1-inch boiling water. Place on the bottom rack of the oven. Place bread in oven and bake for 30 to 40 minutes, or until crust is firm and sounds hollow when thumped. Let cool for 10 minutes before removing from baking sheet. Cool on racks.
Makes 1 or 2 loaves.

Basic Sourdough Bread

Bake this versatile white loaf plain, or try any of the four following recipe variations

1-1/2 cups warm water, 110F (45C)

2-1/2 teaspoons active dry yeast

1 tablespoon sugar

1 cup sourdough starter

1/2 cup butter or margarine, melted

6-1/2 to 7-1/2 cups bread flour

1 teaspoon salt

In a large mixing bowl combine the warm water, yeast and sugar. Stir and let stand for 10 minutes. Stir in sourdough starter and melted butter or margarine. Mix in one half the bread flour and salt. Gradually add enough of the remaining bread flour to make a soft dough. Turn dough out onto a lightly floured smooth surface. Clean and grease the mixing bowl, set aside. Knead the dough for about 10 minutes until smooth and elastic. Place dough in greased bowl, turning to coat all sides. Cover and let rise until double in size, about 1 hour. Grease two 9" x 5" loaf pans. Punch dough down and shape into 2 loaves, Place in prepared pan. Cover and let rise until double in size, about 1 hour. Preheat oven to 350F (175C). Bake for 30 to 35 minutes or until crust is firm and sounds hollow when thumped. Let cool for 10 minutes before removing from pans. Cool on racks. Makes 2 loaves.

Quick Sourdough Bread —Food-Processor Method

Mixing and kneading bread dough in your food processor is an easy way to get a perfect loaf of bread. Most food processors can mix 1 loaf of bread at a time. Larger ones can mix and knead 2 loaves at a time.

2 cups all-purpose or bread flour
1/4 cup butter or margarine
1-3/4 cups sourdough starter
1 teaspoon active dry yeast
1 tablespoon sugar
1 teaspoon salt

Place the plastic bread-kneading blade in the food processor. Add the flour and butter or margarine, turn the food processor on until the butter or margarine is completely mixed in. Pour in the sourdough starter, yeast, sugar and salt. Turn the machine on and let it run until the dough is smooth and gathered into a large ball. If the dough is too damp and sticky, add more flour 1/4 cup at a time until it gathers into a ball as the machine is running. If the dough is too dry, add water by tablespoons until dough gathers into a ball. When the dough is the proper consistency, turn the food processor on to knead the dough for 60 seconds. Place the dough in a greased bowl, cover loosely with plastic wrap. When the dough has doubled in size, about 1 hour, punch it down to remove the air bubbles. Shape it into a loaf and place in a greased 9" X 5"inch loaf pan. Let rise about one hour longer or until doubled in size. Bake in a preheated 350F (175C) oven for 30 minutes, or until the top is golden brown and the loaf sounds hollow when thumped with your finger. Makes 1 loaf.

Onion-Cheddar Double Braid

So yummy you will want to make it over and over again.

Basic Sourdough Bread Recipe, page 34

1 medium onion, chopped

2 tablespoons butter or margarine

6 oz. cheddar cheese, shredded

Prepare Basic Bread Dough up to the first kneading. In a medium sauté pan cook the onion in the butter or margarine until soft and translucent. Set aside to cool. Mix cooled onion mixture and cheese into the dough. Turn dough out onto a lightly floured smooth surface. Clean and grease the mixing bowl, set aside. Knead dough for about 10 minutes until smooth and elastic. Place dough in greased bowl, turning to coat all sides. Cover and let double in size, about 1 hour. Grease a large baking sheet. Punch dough down.

To shape into a double braid, divide dough into 4 equal parts. Divide one part into 3 equal parts, set aside. Shape each of the 3 large portions into 12-inch-long ropes. Place the 3 large ropes on the prepared baking sheet parallel to each other. Start in the middle and braid out to each end. Pinch ends to secure. Do the same with the 3 small ropes. Place small braid on center top of large braid. I use long bamboo picks to secure top braid so it won't slide as bread rises. They can be removed after baking. Cover and let rise until double, about 1 hour. Preheat oven to 375F (190C). Bake for 30 to 40 minutes until golden brown. Makes 1 loaf.

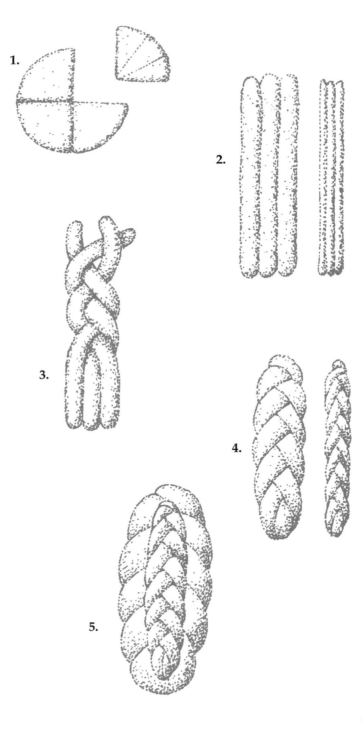

1.

2.

3.

4.

5.

Walnut-Raisin Twist Ring

This bread can also be baked in two greased tube or bundt pans.

Basic Sourdough Bread Recipe, page 34

1 cup raisins

1 cup dried apples, chopped

1 cup warm water

1 teaspoon cinnamon

1/2 teaspoon ground nutmeg

1 cup walnuts, coarsely chopped

Prepare Basic Bread Dough up to kneading point. Plump raisins and apples in warm water for 15 minutes. Drain. Mix in drained raisins, apples, cinnamon, nutmeg and walnuts into dough. Turn dough out onto a lightly floured smooth surface. Clean and grease the mixing bowl, set aside. Knead the dough for about 10 minutes until smooth and elastic. Place dough in greased bowl, turning to coat all sides. Cover and let rise until double in size, about 1 hour. Punch dough down. Divide dough in two. Shape each half into a long rope about 20 inches long. Cut each in half lengthwise. Lay two ropes next to each other and twist 5 or 6 times. Repeat with remaining two ropes. Bend the twists into a circle, matching ends to form a continuous circle. Grease 2 large baking sheets. Place rings on baking sheets to let rise until doubled in size, about 1 hour. Preheat oven to 375F (190C). Bake for 30 minutes, until golden brown. Makes 2 rings.

Parmesan-Oregano Pinwheel

Warm and rich in Italian flavors. Serve with your favorite pasta.

Basic Sourdough Bread Recipe, page 34

6 tablespoons butter, melted

5 oz. Parmesan cheese, grated

2 teaspoons dried-leaf oregano

1 teaspoon dried-leaf basil

Prepare Basic Bread Dough recipe to where it is ready to be shaped. Grease 2 large baking sheets. Divide dough in two. Roll each half into an 11" x 5" rectangle. Brush each with melted butter and sprinkle with Parmesan cheese, oregano and basil. Starting with the longest side, roll up dough jelly-roll fashion. Place on baking sheets.

Cut crosswise almost all the way through each roll at 1-inch intervals (to make circles). Curl dough around into a circle and fan out each cut piece, laying each circle down halfway on top of the one underneath all the way around. Cover and let rise until doubled, about 1 hour. Preheat oven to 375F (190C). Bake for 30 minutes or until golden brown. Makes 2 loaves.

Bread Bouquet

Bread dough is cut into large flower shapes. When baked it looks like a bouquet.

Basic Sourdough Bread Recipe, page 34

Prepare dough up to where it is ready to be shaped. Divide dough into 6 equal pieces. Shape each into a smooth ball and flatten slightly, pinching off a 1/2-inch piece from the bottom of each. Using a sharp knife, cut 6 1-1/2-inch slits into the edges of each ball to create a flower shape. Divide each of the small 1/2-inch pieces of dough into 4 or 5 small balls. Press a thumbsize dent into the center of each of the flowers. Place small balls into the center dent. Grease a large baking sheet. On the prepared baking sheet place 5 of the flowers in a circle with the petals just touching. Brush the underside of the 6th with the egg glaze and place in the center on top. Let rise until almost double in size. Brush entire bouquet with egg wash. Preheat the oven to 375F (190C). Bake in preheated oven for 30 minutes or until golden brown. Makes 1 large bouquet.

Egg Wash Glaze
1 egg
2 tablespoons water

Mix egg with water.

Multi- and Single-Grain Breads

Combining different grains such as wheat, rye or buckwheat in bread baking creates interesting flavors and texture. Wheat flour has the greatest ability to create gluten when kneaded with a liquid. This is why the majority of breads we eat are made from wheat flour.

By using at least 50 percent wheat flour in a recipe you can use other types of flours and grains to create your own masterpiece loaves. See pages 6-9 in the Introduction to learn about other types of flour.

If you have tasted a loaf of bread that you really enjoyed, inquire as to what type of flour was used. You should be able to bake a similar loaf by following one of these recipes. The Honey-Wheat Bread recipe is an adaptation of a local bakery's bread that I love for toast in the morning. A wide variety of flours and grains can be found at specialty markets and health-food stores. You can substitute one or more types of flour in any of these recipes. Just keep the overall measurement the same and remember to use at least 50 percent wheat flour—either white or whole-wheat will work fine.

Oatmeal-Molasses Bread

Loaves can also be baked in two 9" x 5" loaf pans. Honey can be substituted for molasses.

1 cup warm milk or water, 110F (45C)

1 tablespoon active dry yeast

1/3 cup molasses

1/4 cup vegetable oil

1 cup sourdough starter

1 cup rolled oats, regular or quick-cooking

3 to 4 cups bread flour

2 cups whole-wheat flour

2 teaspoons salt

1/4 cup rolled oats, regular or quick-cooking

In a large mixing bowl combine the warm milk, yeast and molasses. Stir and let stand for 10 minutes. Mix in sourdough starter, oil, 1 cup rolled oats, one half the bread flour and all whole-wheat flour and salt. Gradually add the remaining bread flour to make a soft dough. Turn dough out onto a lightly floured surface. Clean and grease the mixing bowl, set aside. Knead the dough for 10 minutes until smooth and elastic. Place dough in greased bowl, turning to coat all sides. Cover and let rise until double in size, about 1-1/2 hours. Grease a large baking sheet. Punch dough down and shape into a large oval about 9" x 5". Brush the top with water and sprinkle with 1/4 cup oats. Place on baking sheet. Cover and let rise until double in size, about 1 hour. Preheat oven to 375F (190C). Bake for 40 to 45 minutes, or until crust is firm and sounds hollow when thumped. Let cool for 10 minutes before removing from pan. Cool on a rack. Makes 1 loaf.

Pumpernickel Bread

The dark-brown color we associate with pumpernickel often comes from adding coffee or cocoa to the bread. Raisins can be used in place of caraway seeds.

1/2 cup warm coffee, 110F (45C)

1 tablespoon active dry yeast

1/3 cup molasses

3/4 cup sourdough starter

2 tablespoons butter or margarine, melted

2 to 3 cups bread flour

2 cups rye flour

1-1/2 tablespoons caraway seeds

2 teaspoons salt

In a large mixing bowl combine the warm coffee, yeast and molasses. Stir and let stand for 10 minutes. Mix in sourdough starter, butter or margarine, one half the bread flour, rye flour, caraway seeds and salt. Gradually add enough of the remaining bread flour to make a soft dough. Turn dough out onto a lightly floured smooth surface. Clean and grease the mixing bowl, set aside. Knead the dough for about 10 minutes until smooth and elastic. Place dough in greased bowl, turning to coat all sides. Cover and let rise until double in size, about 1-1/2 hours. Grease a baking sheet. Punch dough down and shape into a 3-inch-high round. Place on baking sheet. Cover and let rise until double in size, about 1 hour. Preheat oven to 350F (175C). Bake for 40 to 50 minutes, or until crust is firm and sounds hollow when thumped. Let cool for 10 minutes before removing from pans. Cool on rack. Makes 1 loaf.

Oatmeal Bread

To make oat flour, place quick or regular rolled oats in a food processor. Use the steel knife blade and process until reduced to a fine flour.

1-1/2 cups warm milk, 110F (45C)

1 tablespoon active dry yeast

1 tablespoon sugar

1 cup sourdough starter

2 tablespoons vegetable oil

3 to 3-1/2 cups bread flour

2 cups oat flour

1-1/2 teaspoons salt

1/4 cup oats for top of bread

In a large mixing bowl combine the warm milk, yeast and sugar. Stir and let stand for 10 minutes. Mix in sourdough starter, oil and one half the bread flour and all the oat flour and salt. Gradually add enough of the remaining bread flour to make a soft dough. Turn dough out onto a lightly floured smooth surface. Clean and grease the mixing bowl, set aside. Knead the dough for about 10 minutes until smooth and elastic. Place dough in greased bowl, turning to coat all sides. Cover and let rise until double in size, about 1-1/2 hours.

Grease two 9″ x 5″ baking pans. Punch dough down and shape into 2 loaves. Place in prepared pans. Brush top with water and sprinkle with oats. Cover loosely and let rise until double in size, about 1 hour. Preheat oven to 350F (175C). Bake for 30 to 40 minutes, or until crust is firm and sounds hollow when thumped. Let cool for 10 minutes before removing from pans. Cool on racks. Makes 2 loaves.

Variation: **Oatmeal Currant Bread**
Mix in 1-1/2 cups dried currants into dough before first rising.

Brioche

The classic Brioche shape is a round loaf with fluted sides and a round top knot. If you make it loaf shape, the rich flavor and texture of Brioche will be just as good and it will be easier to slice for sandwiches.

2 tablespoons warm water, 110F (45C)

2 tablespoons active dry yeast

1 teaspoon sugar

1/2 cup sourdough starter

3 eggs

1/2 cup butter or margarine, melted

3 to 3-1/2 cups bread flour

1 teaspoon salt

In a large mixing bowl combine the warm water, yeast and sugar. Stir and let stand for 10 minutes. Mix in sourdough starter, eggs, butter or margerine and one half the bread flour and salt. Gradually add enough of the remaining bread flour to make a soft dough. Turn dough out onto a lightly floured smooth surface. Clean and grease the mixing bowl, set aside. Knead the dough for about 10 minutes until smooth and elastic. Place dough in greased bowl, turning to coat all sides. Cover and let rise until double in size, about 1 hour. Grease an 8-inch Brioche pan or a 9" x 5" loaf pan. Punch dough down. To make the Brioche shape, pull off an egg-size piece of dough, roll into a teardrop shape, set aside. Shape remaining dough into a smooth ball. Place dough into Brioche pan. Press your finger down into the center of the ball, knuckle-deep. Press the teardrop shape piece of dough into the indentation, pointed end down. For loaf pan, shape entire loaf of dough into an 8" x 3" rectangle and place in pan. Cover and let rise until double in size, about 1 hour. Brush top of loaf with egg glaze. Preheat oven to 375F (190C). Bake for 30 to 40 minutes, or until crust is firm and golden brown. Let cool for 10 minutes before removing from pans. Cool on racks. Makes 1 loaf.

Egg Glaze

1 egg
2 tablespoons water

Mix egg with water.

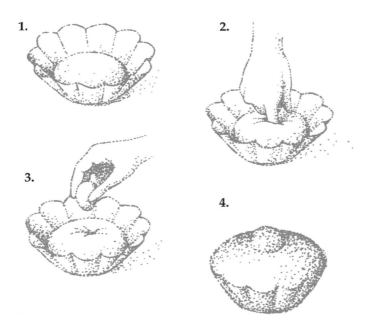

Creating the classic Brioche.

Rosemary-Raisin Sandwich Bread

This aromatic bread is wonderful toasted, but my favorite is to use it for chicken-salad sandwiches.

1-1/4 cups warm milk, 110F (45C)

2 teaspoons sugar

2-1/2 teaspoons active dry yeast

1 cup sourdough starter

1/2 cup butter or margarine, melted and cooled

1 teaspoon salt

**3 tablespoons fresh rosemary, finely chopped
    or 1 tablespoon dried rosemary leaves**

1 cup raisins

7 cups all-purpose or bread flour

In a large mixing bowl, combine the milk, sugar and yeast. Let set for 10 minutes. Mix in starter, margarine or butter, salt, rosemary, raisins and 5 cups of flour. Gradually mix in the remaining flour 1 cup at a time until dough is no longer sticky, adding more flour if necessary. Turn dough out onto a floured surface and knead for 10 minutes. Dough should be smooth and elastic. Place in a greased bowl, cover with plastic wrap and let rise until double, about 1-1/2 hours. Punch dough down to remove most of the air bubbles and divide in half. Grease two 8" x 4" loaf pans. Shape loaves to fit and place in pans with smooth side up. Cover again and let rise until almost double in size. Preheat oven to 350F (175C). Bake in preheated oven for about 30 minutes. Crust should be golden brown and loaf should sound hollow when thumped with your finger. Makes 2 loaves.

Honey-Wheat Bread

I've made this recipe for years and it's still my favorite for toasting. For texture and goodness add 1/4 cup sunflower seeds.

1/2 cup warm milk, 110F (45C)

1 tablespoon active dry yeast

1/4 cup honey

3/4 cup sourdough starter

1 egg

1/4 cup butter or margarine, melted

1-1/2 to 2 cups bread flour

2 cups whole-wheat flour

1-1/2 teaspoons salt

In a large mixing bowl combine the warm milk, yeast, and honey. Stir and let stand for 10 minutes. Mix in sourdough starter, egg and butter or margarine. Mix in one half the bread flour with all of the whole-wheat flour and salt. Gradually add enough of the remaining bread flour to make a soft dough. Turn dough out onto a lightly floured smooth surface. Clean and grease the mixing bowl, set aside. Knead the dough for about 10 minutes until smooth and elastic. Place dough in greased bowl, turning to coat all sides. Cover and let rise until double in size, about 1 hour. Grease a 9" x 5" loaf pan. Punch dough down and shape into a loaf. Place in prepared pan. Cover and let rise until double in size, about 1 hour. Preheat oven to 375F (190C). Bake for 40 minutes, or until crust is firm and golden brown and sounds hollow when thumped. Let cool for 10 minutes before removing from pan. Cool on rack. Makes 1 loaf.

Squaw-Bread Rolls

I like to use this roll recipe for hamburger buns. Shape them to a 3-inch diameter and flatten to about 1-1/2 inches high before baking.

1/4 cup warm water, 110F (45C)

2 teaspoons active dry yeast

1/3 cup molasses

1 cup sourdough starter

1/4 cup butter or margarine, melted

2 to 2-1/2 cups bread flour

1-3/4 cups whole wheat flour

1 teaspoon salt

In a large mixing bowl combine the warm water, yeast and molasses. Stir and let stand for 10 minutes. Mix in the sourdough starter and melted butter or margarine. Mix in one half the bread flour and all the whole-wheat flour and salt. Gradually add enough of the remaining bread flour to make a soft dough. Turn dough out onto a lightly floured smooth surface. Clean and grease the mixing bowl, set aside. Knead the dough for about 10 minutes until smooth and elastic. Place dough in greased bowl, turning to coat all sides. Cover and let rise until double in size, about 1 hour. Grease a large baking sheet. Punch dough down and shape into 2-inch balls for dinner size rolls and 3-inch balls for hamburger buns. Slightly flatten the hamburger roll balls. Place on prepared baking sheet. Cover and let rise until double in size, about 30 minutes. Preheat oven to 375F (190C). Bake for 15 to 20 minutes until crust is firm. Let cool for 10 minutes removing from baking sheet. Cool on racks. Makes 18 dinner rolls or 12 hamburger buns.

Pita Bread

Whole-wheat flour can be substituted for half the bread flour to make whole-wheat Pitas. Cut baked pitas (also called pocket bread) in half crosswise and fill with your favorite sandwich ingredients. They also make great appetizer dippers. Cut pitas into pie-shaped wedges.

3/4 cup warm water, 110F (45C)

2 teaspoons active dry yeast

1 teaspoon sugar

3/4 cup sourdough starter

2 tablespoons oil

4 to 5 cups bread flour

1 teaspoon salt

Cornmeal

In a large mixing bowl combine the warm water, yeast and sugar. Stir and let stand for 10 minutes. Mix in sourdough starter, oil, one half the bread flour and the salt. Gradually add enough of the remaining bread flour to make a soft dough. Turn dough out onto a lightly floured smooth surface. Clean and grease the mixing bowl, set aside. Knead the dough for about 10 minutes until smooth and elastic. Place dough in greased bowl, turning to coat all sides. Cover and let rise until double in size, about 1 hour. Preheat oven to 425F (220C). Divide dough into 10 equal pieces and shape into balls. Using a rolling pin, roll balls into 8-inch circles. Sprinkle 2 large baking sheets with cornmeal. Place pita rounds on baking sheets so they have 1 inch between. Bake in batches in preheated oven for about 5 to 10 minutes, until dry and slightly puffed. Place on racks to cool. Store in airtight container to soften. Makes 10 pitas.

Sally Lunn

This light sweet bread was first introduced in 18th century England by a peddler named Sally Lunn.

1-1/4 cups warm water, 110F (45C)

1 tablespoon active dry yeast

1 cup sourdough starter

1/2 cup sugar

4 to 5 cups bread flour

1/4 cup butter or margarine, melted

2 eggs

1 teaspoon salt

In a large mixing bowl combine the warm water, yeast, sourdough starter and sugar. Stir and let stand for 10 minutes. Mix in one half the bread flour and salt. Gradually add enough of the remaining bread flour to make a soft dough. Turn dough out onto a lightly floured smooth surface. Clean and grease the mixing bowl, set aside. Knead the dough for about 10 minutes until smooth and elastic. Place dough in greased bowl, turning to coat all sides. Cover and let rise until double in size, about 1 hour. Grease a baking sheet. Punch dough down, divide in half and shape each half into a large bun shape. Place on prepared baking sheet. Cover and let rise until double in size, about 1 hour. Preheat oven to 350F (175C). Bake for 30 to 40 minutes, or until crust is golden brown. If top begins to brown too quickly cover with a tent made of foil. Let cool for 10 minutes before removing from baking sheet. Cool on racks. Makes 2 loaves.

Fruit and Nut Breads

Nothing is more simply elegant than the rich earthy flavor and texture of home-baked breads. However, once you start adding toasted pecans or a few chopped dried apricots or raisins to your loaves, you will find that the possible combinations are endless.

The markets and specialty food stores carry a jewel-like array of dried fruits such as apricots, dates, strawberries, blueberries, cherries and cranberries. Dried, frozen and chopped fruits and nuts can be added to any bread recipe without altering any of the other ingredients, which makes bread baking even more interesting.

My Blueberry Muffin Mix can be made with frozen raspberries or chopped fresh strawberries depending upon the season. While most breads taste just right for any season, some are kept for special times during the year. Grandma Kriedman Stollen is the perfect example of a holiday bread that could be made anytime during the year, but it remains special because in the Kriedman home it is only made once a year.

Fruit and nut breads in this chapter are often served for breakfast which suggests to me that making them ahead of time, freezing and then reheating just in time to serve is a great idea. Make a double batch: eat one now and freeze one for future use. If wrapped tightly, breads can be frozen for up to 6 months without losing their fresh flavor.

Grandma Kriedman's Stollen

This lady was a friend's grandmother. She must have been a wonderful baker. Perhaps your grandmother's kitchen was filled with the aroma of freshly baked bread, too. My friend's grandmother baked the stollen in a tube pan. For a more classical shape, instead of rolling jelly-roll style, fold the circle of dough in half over the filling, leaving about 1" at the edge.

3/4 cup warm milk, 110F (45C)

1 tablespoon active dry yeast

3/4 cup sugar

1/2 cup sourdough starter

3 eggs, separated

3/4 to 1 cup all-purpose flour

1 cup butter, room temperature

1 teaspoon salt

1/2 cup almonds, chopped

3/4 cup raisins

In a large mixing bowl combine the warm milk, yeast and 2 tablespoons of the sugar. Beat in sourdough starter and egg yolks. In a separate bowl cut together 3/4 cup flour, butter and salt. Mix liquid and flour mixture, adding more flour if necessary to form a smooth dough. Clean and grease the mixing bowl, set aside. Turn dough out onto a lightly floured smooth surface. Knead for about 10 minutes until smooth and elastic. Place dough in greased bowl, turning to coat all sides. Cover and let rise for about 1-1/2 hours, until double in size. Beat egg whites until soft peaks form, gradually add remaining sugar. Roll dough out into a circle, 1 inch thick. Preheat oven to 375F (190C) and grease a 9-inch tube pan. Spread top of dough circle with egg whites and sprinkle evenly with almonds and raisins. Roll up jelly-roll style and place in tube pan. Cover lightly and let rise about 1 hour. Bake in prepared oven for 30 to 40 minutes until top is golden brown. Cool on rack; top with Powdered Sugar Glaze. Makes 1 stollen.

Powdered Sugar Glaze

If you like, reserve a tablespoon each of raisins and almonds to sprinkle on top of this glaze.

1/2 cup powdered sugar, sifted
1 tablespoon milk or lemon juice

Stir ingredients together until perfectly smooth. Spread on cooled stollen. Top with a few almonds and raisins.

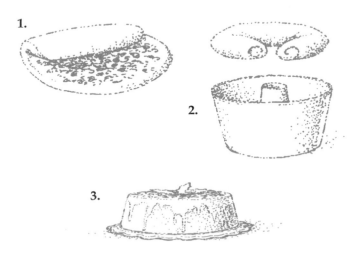

Cranberry-Pecan Bread Pudding

Originally bread pudding was a way to use up leftover bread. But it's such a favorite of mine I find that I bake bread just so I can use it in pudding.

6 slices dry day-old bread

4 cups milk

4 eggs

3/4 cup sugar

3/4 teaspoon ground cinnamon

1/4 teaspoon ground nutmeg

1 teaspoon vanilla extract

1/2 cup dried cranberries or dried blueberries, fresh chopped apple or raisins

1/2 cup chopped pecans

Preheat the oven to 325F (165C). Grease an 8-inch square baking pan. Cut the bread into 1-inch squares, set aside. In a large mixing bowl whip together the milk, eggs, sugar, cinnamon, nutmeg and vanilla. Stir into the bread together with cranberries or whatever dried fruits you choose and pecans. Let stand for 15 minutes, stirring twice so bread absorbs most of the liquid. Pour mixture into prepared pan and bake in preheated oven for 1 hour. Top should be puffed up and light golden brown. Serve with Maple Brown-Sugar Sauce, if desired. (Recipe on next page.) Makes 6 servings.

Maple Brown-Sugar Sauce

1/2 cup brown sugar

1/4 cup water

1/4 cup maple flavored syrup

2 tablespoons butter or margarine

1/8 teaspoon vanilla extract

In a small saucepan combine the brown sugar, water, syrup and butter or margarine. Bring to a boil and boil for 2 minutes. Remove from heat. Stir in vanilla. Makes 3/4 cup sauce.

Apricot-Cranberry Bread

Try this bread for a turkey sandwich, or cut thick slices for a marvelous French toast.

1/4 cup warm water, 110F (45C)

1 tablespoon active dry yeast

1/3 cup sugar

1 cup sourdough starter

1 cup orange juice

1/3 cup butter or margarine, melted

2 eggs

3 to 4 cups bread flour

3/4 cup dried apricots, finely chopped

3/4 cup dried cranberries

2 tablespoons grated orange peel

1 teaspoon salt

1 teaspoon vanilla extract

In a large mixing bowl combine the warm water, yeast and 1 tablespoon sugar. Stir and let stand for 10 minutes. Stir in remaining sugar, sourdough starter, orange juice, butter or margarine and eggs. Mix in one half the bread flour and all remaining ingredients. Gradually add enough of the remaining bread flour to make a soft dough. Turn dough out onto a lightly floured smooth surface. Clean and grease the mixing bowl, set aside. Knead the dough for about 10 minutes until smooth and elastic. Place dough in greased bowl, turning to coat all sides. Cover and let rise until double in size, about 1 hour.

Grease two 8" x 4" pans. Punch dough down and shape
into 2 loaves. Place in prepared pans. Cover and let rise
until double in size, about 1 hour. Preheat oven to 350F
(170C). Bake for 30 to 40 minutes until crust is golden
brown and sounds hollow when thumped. Let cool for 10
minutes before removing from pans. Cool on racks. Makes
2 loaves.

Upside-Down Apricot Coffeecake

For a different flavor, use 1-1/2 cups of coarsely chopped apples in place of the apricots.

Topping:

2 (16-oz.) cans apricot or pear halves, drained

1/3 cup brown sugar

1/4 cup all-purpose flour

1/2 teaspoon ground cinnamon

1/8 teaspoon ground nutmeg

1/4 cup butter or margarine

1/2 cup chopped pecans

Cake Batter:

3/4 cup sourdough starter

1-1/4 cups all-purpose flour

1/3 cup sugar

1-1/2 teaspoons baking powder

1/4 teaspoon salt

1/4 cup butter or margarine, melted

1 egg, slightly beaten

1 teaspoon vanilla extract

Preheat the oven to 350F (175C). Generously grease an 11"x 7" baking dish. Place apricot or pear halves cut side up in the bottom of the baking dish. Prepare the topping: In a medium mixing bowl combine the brown sugar, flour, cinnamon and nutmeg. Work in 1/4 cup butter or margarine until crumbly. Mix in the pecans and sprinkle mixture over apricots. To prepare the cake batter: Mix all cake batter ingredients until well blended. Spoon batter evenly over apricot mixture. Bake in preheated oven for 50 to 60 minutes or until golden brown. Remove from oven. Cut around edges of the cake with a knife to loosen. Place serving platter over top of baking dish and invert. Gently remove pan. Makes 8 to 10 servings.

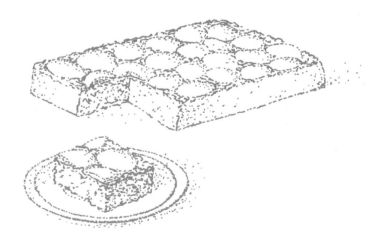

Cranberry-Orange Oat Bread

Try using a couple of slices of this bread for your next chicken sandwich. Oat flour can be made by finely chopping rolled oats, (regular or quick) in your food processor or blender.

1-1/3 cups warm milk, 110F (45C)

1 tablespoon active dry yeast

1 tablespoon sugar

1 cup sourdough starter

1/4 cup vegetable oil

4 to 4-1/2 cups bread flour

3 cups oat flour

1-1/2 teaspoons salt

1 cup dried cranberries

1 cup dried apricots, finely chopped

In a large mixing bowl combine the warm milk, yeast and sugar. Stir and let stand for 10 minutes. Mix in the sourdough starter, oil, one half the bread flour, all of the oat flour, salt, cranberries and apricots. Gradually add enough of the remaining bread flour to form a soft dough. Turn the dough out onto a lightly floured smooth surface. Knead dough for about 10 minutes until smooth and elastic. Place in the greased mixing bowl. Cover and let rise until double in size, about 1 hour. Grease two 9" x 5" loaf pans. Punch dough down and shape into two equal loaves. Place in prepared pans. Cover and let rise until double in size. Preheat the oven to 375F (190C). Bake for 30 to 40 minutes or until crust is golden brown. Let cool for 10 minutes before removing from pans. Cool on racks. Makes 2 loaves.

Scones

Scones are traditionally served with jam and Devonshire cream. Because Devonshire Cream isn't readily available in North America, I substitute whipped cream.

2 cups all-purpose flour

2 teaspoons baking powder

2 tablespoons sugar

1/4 teaspoon salt

1/3 cup butter or margarine

1/2 cup sourdough starter

1 egg

2 tablespoons milk

1/3 cup currants or light raisins

1 tablespoon grated orange peel

Preheat the oven to 425F (220C). In a large mixing bowl or food processor combine the flour, baking powder, sugar and salt. Cut in the butter or margarine until completely mixed. Add the sourdough starter, egg, milk, currants or raisins and orange peel. Mix completely. If you are using a food processor, let the machine run about 15 seconds to lightly knead the dough. If mixing by hand, turn the dough out onto a lightly floured smooth surface. Knead 12 or 15 times, just until the dough is smooth. Roll dough out 3/4 inch thick. Cut into twelve 2-inch circles. A drinking glass works well as a cutter. Place the circles on an ungreased baking sheet. Bake in a preheated oven for about 15 minutes until light golden brown on top. Makes 12 scones.

Eccles Cakes

*While on vacation in London, my children loved walking
around the corner to the bread shop every morning to buy
these traditional English cakes fresh from the oven.*

2 cups all-purpose flour

2 teaspoons baking powder

3 tablespoons sugar

1/4 teaspoon salt

1/3 cup butter or margarine

1/2 cup sourdough starter

2 eggs, beaten

2 tablespoons milk

1/4 cup currants

1/4 teaspoon ground cinnamon

2 teaspoons coarse decorating sugar or regular sugar

2 tablespoons water

Preheat the oven to 425F (220C). In a large mixing bowl
combine the flour, baking powder, 2 tablespoons sugar
and salt. Cut the butter or margarine into small pieces
and using a fork blend it into the flour mixture. Stir in
the sourdough starter, 1 egg beaten and milk until it
forms a smooth dough. Turn the dough out onto a lightly
floured smooth surface. Knead 20 to 30 times until dough
is smooth.

Grease a large baking sheet. Roll dough out 1/2-inch thick.
Cut into eight 3-inch circles. A drinking glass works well
as a cutter. Place 2 inches apart on prepared baking sheet.
In a small bowl mix the currants, 1 tablespoon sugar and
cinnamon. Spoon currant mixture equally into center of
each circle. Beat remaining egg with 2 tablespoons water.
Brush outer edge of each circle with mixture. Pull opposite
sides of the dough up to the center and pinch to hold.
Brush with egg mixture. Sprinkle with decorating sugar.
Bake in preheated oven for about 15 minutes until golden
brown. Makes 8 cakes.

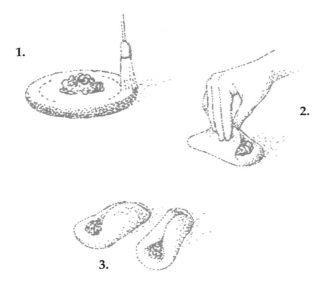

Cinnamon-Pecan Coffeecake

This is the best coffeecake I have ever made. Keep one on hand in the freezer and you'll always be ready for unexpected guests.

1/3 cup brown sugar, packed

1/3 cup granulated sugar

1 teaspoon cinnamon

3/4 cup chopped pecans

3/4 cup butter or margarine

1 cup granulated sugar

2 eggs

1 cup sourdough starter

1/4 cup milk

2 cups all-purpose flour

1 teaspoon baking soda

1 teaspoon baking powder

1/2 teaspoon salt

1 teaspoon vanilla extract

Preheat oven to 325F (165C). Grease a 9-inch tube pan. In a small mixing bowl, combine the brown sugar, 1/3 cup granulated sugar, cinnamon and pecans, set aside. Using an electric mixer, cream the butter and 1 cup sugar. Mix in eggs, sourdough starter, milk, flour, soda, baking powder, salt and vanilla. Mix until light, about 3 minutes. Pour half the batter into the prepared pan, spreading evenly over the bottom. Sprinkle with half the pecan mixture. Pour in remaining batter and top with remaining pecan mixture. Bake in preheated oven for 40 minutes. Let cool in pan 10 minutes. To remove coffee cake from pan, place a plate upside down over pan. Invert pan and plate. Remove pan. Place a serving plate on top of coffee cake, invert again. Remove top plate. Makes 8 servings.

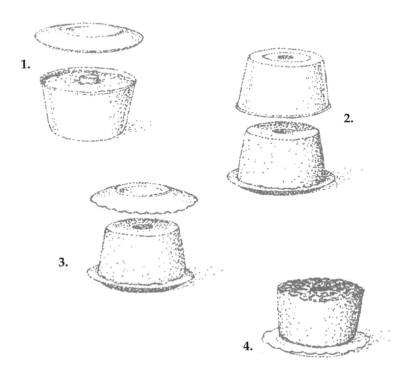

1.

2.

3.

4.

Hot Cross Buns

A traditional Easter favorite, but just as tasty all year 'round.

1/3 cup warm water, 110F (45C)

2 teaspoons active dry yeast

3 tablespoons sugar

3/4 cup sourdough starter

3 tablespoons butter or margarine

2 to 2-1/2 cups bread flour

1/2 teaspoon salt

1/2 cup golden raisins

1/2 cup assorted candied fruit, coarsely chopped
Powdered Sugar Glaze, page 55

In a large mixing bowl combine the warm water, yeast and sugar. Stir and let stand for 10 minutes. Mix in sourdough starter, butter or margarine, one half the bread flour, salt, raisins and candied fruit. Gradually add enough of the remaining bread flour to make a soft dough. Turn dough out onto a lightly floured smooth surface. Clean and grease the mixing bowl, set aside. Knead the dough for about 10 minutes until smooth and elastic. Place dough in greased bowl, turning to coat all sides. Cover and let rise until double in size, about 1 hour. Grease 1 large baking sheet. Punch dough down and shape into 12 balls. Place on prepared baking sheet. Cover and let rise until double in size, about 30 minutes. Preheat oven to 375F (190C). Bake for 20 minutes, or until crust is firm and golden. Cool on racks. When completely cooled, make a cross on the top of each bun with Powdered Sugar Icing. Makes 12 rolls.

Blueberry-Muffin Mix

This is a basic muffin recipe. You can add up to 1 cup of raisins, all-bran cereal, dried cherries or cranberries to vary the taste.

1/2 cup sourdough starter

2/3 cup milk

1 egg

2 tablespoons oil or melted butter

2 cups all-purpose flour

1/3 cup sugar

1 tablespoon baking powder

1/4 teaspoon salt

1 cup fresh or frozen blueberries, raspberries or cherries

Streusel topping

Preheat the oven to 400F (205C). Grease 6 extra large muffin cups. In a large mixing bowl mix the sourdough starter, milk, egg and oil. Stir in the flour, sugar, baking powder and salt just until mixed. Stir in the blueberries or combination of flavoring ingredients. Spoon dough into muffin cups 2/3 full. Sprinkle tops with Streusel topping, if desired. Bake in preheated oven about 20 minutes. Makes 6 large muffins.

Streusel Topping
1/3 cup brown sugar
1/4 cup all-purpose flour
2 tablespoons butter or margarine
1/8 teaspoon ground cinnamon

In a small mixing bowl mix all ingredients until crumbly. Spoon over muffins just before baking.

Savory Breads

The easiest way to define *savory* is to say it is the opposite of sweet. Aromatic herbs, flavorful cheeses and interesting vegetable flavors are the keys to these savory recipes. Appetizers, lunches and dinners are where these breads shine. Try a chicken-salad sandwich served on Cheese Pinwheel Bread for lunch. Or use your best olive oil with just a hint of Balsamic vinegar added and dip in a warm slice of Focaccia, my favorite Italian bread.

Experimenting with the ingredients you add to each loaf keeps bread baking fun. In the Cheese and Chive Biscuits try using goat cheese or feta the second time you make the recipe. I always suggest following a recipe fairly closely the first time you make it. The reason you usually decide to try a recipe is that it sounds good to you. While you are eating, make a mental note as to what you would do or change next time, then write your ideas down next to the recipe for reference next time.

I recommend using fresh herbs when possible. Fortunately most supermarkets carry an assortment of fresh herbs. However, if you must use dried, remember 1 tablespoon dried is equal to 3 tablespoons fresh.

Try changing shapes, make your breads into rolls for a dinner or a free form round instead of a classical loaf pan shape. Creating the look of the bread can be just as interesting as creating the combination of flavors.

Potato Bread

If you don't have leftover mashed potatoes you can quickly make some using instant mashed potatoes. Their addition enhances the texture and provides a delicate flavor.

1/2 cup warm water 110F (45C)

2 teaspoons active dry yeast

2 tablespoons sugar

1 cup sourdough starter

1 cup mashed potatoes

3 tablespoons vegetable oil

1 egg

5 to 6 cups bread flour

2 teaspoons salt

In a large mixing bowl combine the warm water, yeast, sugar and sourdough starter. Stir and let stand for 10 minutes. Stir in the potatoes, oil and egg. Mix in one half the bread flour and the salt. Gradually add enough of the remaining bread flour to make a soft dough. Turn dough out onto a lightly floured smooth surface. Clean and grease the mixing bowl, set aside. Knead the dough for about 10 minutes until smooth and elastic. Place dough in greased bowl, turning to coat all sides. Cover and let rise until double in size, about 1-1/2 hours. Grease two 9" x 5" pans. Punch dough down and shape into two loaves. Place in prepared pans. Cover and let rise until double in size, about 1 hour. Preheat oven to 350F (175C). Bake for 30 minutes, or until crust is firm and sounds hollow when thumped. Let cool for 10 minutes before removing from pans. Cool on racks. Makes 2 loaves.

Miniature Rolled Herb Loaves

Fresh herbs are an important part of this recipe, feel free to use any combination of herbs available. Begin with rosemary, basil, dill, sage or parsley.

3/4 cup warm water, 110F (45C)

1 tablespoon active dry yeast

1 teaspoon sugar

2 eggs

1/4 cup olive oil

1-1/4 cups sourdough starter

5 to 6 cups bread flour

2 teaspoons salt

Olive oil

1/3 cup fresh, finely chopped, marjoram

1/3 cup fresh, finely chopped thyme

In a large mixing bowl combine the warm water, yeast and sugar. Stir and let stand for 10 minutes. Mix in eggs, oil, sourdough starter, one-half the bread flour and the salt. Gradually add enough of the remaining bread flour to make a soft dough. Turn dough out onto a lightly floured smooth surface. Clean and grease the mixing bowl, set aside. Knead the dough for about 10 minutes until smooth and elastic. Place dough in greased bowl, turning to coat all sides. Cover and let rise until double in size, about 1 hour.

Grease a large baking sheet. Punch dough down, divide and shape into 6 equal portions. Roll each portion into a 12″ x 4″ rectangle. Brush each liberally with olive oil and sprinkle with marjoram and thyme. Roll each up tightly starting with the short sides. Place on prepared baking sheet, not touching. Cover and let rise until double in size, about 30 minutes. Preheat oven to 375F (190C). Bake for 15 to 20 minutes, or until crust is firm and golden brown. Let cool for 10 minutes before removing from baking sheet. Cool on racks. Makes 6 small loaves.

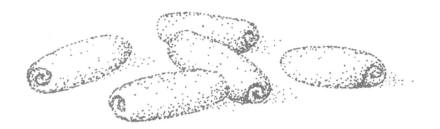

Caraway, Anise and Sesame-Seed Baguettes

These classic shape baguettes are rolled in a mixture of caraway, anise and sesame seeds before baking to give an intriguing flavor to every bite.

1 cup warm milk, 110F (45C)

1 tablespoon active dry yeast

1 teaspoon sugar

1-1/2 cups sourdough starter

5 to 6 cups bread flour

1 teaspoon salt

1/4 cup caraway seeds

1/4 cup sesame seeds

1/4 cup anise seeds

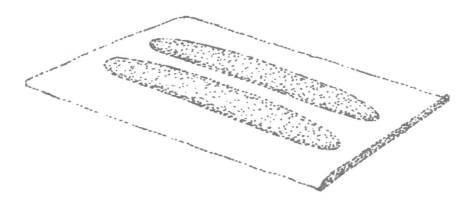

In a large mixing bowl combine the warm water, yeast and sugar. Stir and let stand for 10 minutes. Mix in the sourdough starter and 3 cups bread flour. Cover loosely, and let stand out for 4 hours or overnight. Mixture should be full of bubbles. Gradually mix in the salt and enough of the remaining bread flour to make a soft dough. Turn dough out onto a lightly floured smooth surface. Clean and grease the mixing bowl, set aside. Knead the dough for about 10 minutes until smooth and elastic. Place dough in prepared bowl, turning to coat all sides. Cover and let rise until double in size, about 1 hour. Punch dough down and shape into two 14-inch-long loaves. Sprinkle a baking sheet liberally with a mixture of the sesame, anise and caraway seeds. Place both shaped loaves on the sheet and roll in the seed mixture to coat all sides. Remove any seeds from the baking sheet that did not adhere to the dough. Cover lightly and let rise until double in size, about 45 minutes. Preheat oven to 375F (190C). Bake in preheated oven for about 30 minutes, until golden brown. Makes 2 loaves.

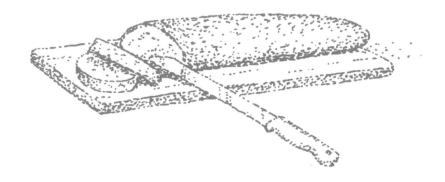

Breadsticks

1 recipe Basic Quick Sourdough Bread—Food-Processor Method, page 35

1 egg

2 tablespoons water

Cracked wheat, sesame seeds or poppy seeds for topping

Prepare bread dough through the first rising. Punch dough down and divide in half. Roll each piece into a 12" x 8" rectangle. Cut each rectangle into strips 8" x 1". For large bread sticks place strips on a greased baking sheet, twisting 4 or 5 times if desired.

For thin breadsticks, roll each strip into a 10-inch-long rope and place on baking sheet. Cover loosely and let rise until doubled in size. Brush with a mixture of the egg and water beaten together. Sprinkle with topping of your choice. Bake in preheated oven, 400F (205C), for 15 to 20 minutes. Makes 24 bread sticks.

Egg Glaze

1 egg

2 tablespoons water

Mix egg with water.

Cheese Pinwheel Bread

This loaf is fun for sandwiches as well as toast. Just remember if you toast it the cheese will get very hot.

1/4 cup warm milk, 110F (45C)

2 tablespoons active dry yeast

1 tablespoon sugar

1-1/2 cups sourdough starter

1 tablespoon oil

3 to 4 cups bread flour

1 teaspoon salt

1/2 cup shredded sharp cheddar or Swiss cheese

1/4 cup Parmesan cheese

1/2 cup green onion stems, finely sliced

In a large mixing bowl combine the warm milk, yeast and sugar. Stir and let stand for 10 minutes. Mix in sourdough starter, oil, one half the bread flour and the salt. Gradually add enough of the remaining bread flour to make a soft dough. Turn dough out onto a lightly floured smooth surface. Clean and grease the mixing bowl, set aside. Knead the dough for about 10 minutes until smooth and elastic. Place dough in greased bowl, turning to coat all sides. Cover and let rise until double in size, about 1 hour.

Grease a 9" x 5" pan. Punch dough down and roll out into a 8" x 12" rectangle. Sprinkle evenly with cheeses and green onions. Roll up jelly-roll fashion beginning on an 8-inch side. Pinch ends and edges to seal. Place in prepared pan. Cover and let rise until double in size, about 1 hour. Preheat oven to 350F (170C). Bake for 50 to 60 minutes, or until crust is firm and sounds hollow when thumped. Let cool for 10 minutes before removing from pan. Cool on rack. Makes 1 loaf.

Focaccia

Serve this Italian flat bread with a small bowl of olive oil and Balsamic vinegar for dipping. Top with sautéed onions, thinly sliced tomatoes and fresh basil leaves.

1/4 cup warm water, 110F (45C)

2 tablespoons active dry yeast

1 tablespoon sugar

1 cup sourdough starter

2 tablespoons olive oil

2-1/4 cups bread flour

1 teaspoon salt

**1 tablespoon fresh rosemary, finely chopped
  or 1 teaspoon dried**

Olive oil

Coarse ground salt

Fresh Toppings:

Sautéed onion

Tomatoes, thinly sliced

Fresh basil leaves

Black olives, sliced

In a large mixing bowl combine the warm water, yeast and sugar. Stir and let stand for 10 minutes. Mix in sourdough starter, oil, one half the bread flour, the salt and rosemary. Gradually add enough of the remaining bread flour to make a soft dough. Turn dough out onto a lightly floured smooth surface. Clean and coat the mixing bowl with olive oil, set aside. Knead the dough for about 10 minutes until smooth and elastic. Place dough in oiled bowl, turning to coat all sides. Cover and let rise until double in size, about 1 hour.

Grease a baking sheet. Punch down dough and shape into a 12" x 12" square. Using your fingers press holes into dough all over the top about 2 inches apart. Place on prepared pan. Cover and let rise until double in size, about 1 hour. Preheat oven to 375F (190C). Brush top of dough with olive oil and sprinkle with coarsely ground salt. Bake for 20 to 30 minutes, or until crust is firm and sounds hollow when thumped. Let cool for 10 minutes before removing from pan. Cool on rack. Garnish with one or more suggested toppings. Makes 1 loaf.

Popovers, Pancakes and Waffles

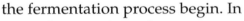

At one time in California's mining history, sourdough pancakes were as popular as sourdough bread is today. The addition of sourdough starter to pancakes gives an extra-yummy flavor. Once you try sourdough pancakes you will want to make sourdough waffles and then crumpets, bagels and popovers.

Sourdough starter in quick-type breads, that is bread products that do not need a rising time, adds flavor and a nice chewy texture. If you do want to make pancakes or waffles leavened solely with sourdough starter, begin the night before and make a sponge out of the starter, plus the liquid and half the flour called for in the recipe. Mix it well, cover and leave out on the counter overnight to let the fermentation process begin. In the morning when you are ready to cook, stir in the remaining flour and flavoring ingredients, but eliminate any baking soda or baking powder, because you won't need it.

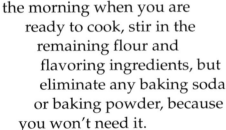

If you want to experiment with the different starters, try the rye or whole-wheat to taste the type of flavor they develop. Use them in the Popover, Crumpet or Pancake recipes; you can taste the different flavors and they will not be overwhelmed or disguised by other ingredients.

Sourdough Pancakes

If you decide to mix and serve these pancakes the same morning they will be tasty, but not quite as sour as those made with overnight batter.

1 cup sourdough starter

1-1/2 cups milk

2 cups all-purpose flour

1 egg

2 teaspoons baking powder

1/2 teaspoon salt

The night before: In a medium mixing bowl stir together the sourdough starter, milk and 1 cup flour. Cover and refrigerate.

Just before serving: Preheat and grease the griddle. To the sourdough mixture beat in the remaining ingredients. Pour batter by 1/4 cupfuls onto heated griddle. Cook about 2 minutes on each side until light golden brown on both sides. Makes about 12 pancakes.

Silver-Dollar Buckwheat Pancakes

Silver-dollar pancakes are called that because they are about the size of a silver dollar.

1 egg

1 cup milk

3/4 cup sourdough starter

2 tablespoons vegetable oil

3/4 cup buckwheat flour

3/4 cup all-purpose flour

3/4 teaspoon baking powder

1/2 teaspoon baking soda

1/2 teaspoon salt

Preheat and oil griddle. In a medium bowl mix the egg, milk and sourdough starter together. Stir in remaining ingredients. Pour batter onto preheated griddle, using 1 tablespoon per pancake. Cook about 1 minute per side or until golden brown. Makes 4 servings.

Whole-Wheat Pancakes or Waffles

Top with applesauce and a few sliced strawberries instead of butter and syrup for a healthy breakfast.

2 eggs

1-1/2 cups milk

2 tablespoons vegetable oil

3/4 cup sourdough starter

1 cup whole-wheat flour

1 cup all-purpose flour

1 teaspoon baking powder

1/2 teaspoon baking soda

1/4 teaspoon salt

2 tablespoons sugar

Preheat waffle baker or griddle. In a medium mixing bowl whip the eggs, milk and oil together. Add remaining ingredients and mix until smooth. Pour into preheated waffle baker by 1/2 cupfuls or onto preheated griddle by 1/4 cupfuls. For pancakes cook about 2 minutes on each side. Makes about 6 waffles or 14 pancakes.

Blue-Cornmeal Waffles

Cornmeal adds a wonderful crisp crunch and color to waffles.
Use white or yellow cornmeal if the blue is not available. Try
serving these with lemon sauce rather than maple syrup.
I think you'll like the combination.

2 eggs

1 cup milk

1 cup sourdough starter

1 cup blue cornmeal

1 cup all-purpose flour

3 tablespoons sugar

1 teaspoon baking powder

1/2 teaspoon baking soda

1/4 cup butter or margarine, melted

Preheat the waffle baker. In a medium mixing bowl
combine the eggs, milk and sourdough starter. Mix in
remaining ingredients until batter is smooth. Pour batter
into preheated waffle baker by 1/2 cupfuls. Bake until
golden brown. Makes about six 8-inch waffles.

Sourdough Popovers

For a different flavor add 1 teaspoon finely chopped basil or green onions to dry ingredients.

6 eggs

3/4 cup milk

1 cup sourdough starter

1/3 cup butter or margarine, melted

1 cup all-purpose flour

1/2 teaspoon salt

Preheat oven to 400F (205C). In a medium mixing bowl beat the eggs until light-colored. Beat in the milk and sourdough starter and melted butter. Stir in the flour and salt. To prevent the popovers from sticking to the baking cups, generously grease the cups, place in hot oven for 5 minutes, then remove and fill. Pour batter equally into prepared custard cups. Place cups on a baking sheet and then into preheated oven. Bake for about 30 to 40 minutes until tall and golden brown. Makes 8 popovers.

This recipe makes 4 cups of batter. For large muffin tins or custard cups, use 1/2 cup batter per cup. For a regular-size muffin tin, use 1/3 cup batter for each popover.

Dutch Pancakes

One of my favorite ways to serve this delicious treat is to sprinkle it liberally with powdered sugar and then squeeze fresh lemon juice over that.

3 eggs

1-1/2 cups milk

3/4 cup sourdough starter

1 cup all-purpose flour

1/4 cup sugar

2 tablespoons vegetable oil

1 teaspoon salt

Preheat oven to 425F (220C). Generously grease a 10-inch skillet with an oven-proof handle. Using an electric mixer or blender mix all ingredients together until smooth. Pour batter into prepared skillet and bake for 10 minutes. Reduce temperature to 350F (175C). Bake until golden brown, about 25 minutes longer. Cut into 6 wedges to serve. Top with Mandarin Strawberry-Fruit Sauce (recipe opposite). Makes 6 servings.

Mandarin Strawberry Fruit Sauce

1 (10-oz.) pkg. frozen strawberry halves, thawed

1 (10-oz.) can Mandarin oranges, drained

1 cup orange juice, about

2 tablespoons sugar

1-1/2 tablespoons cornstarch

1 teaspoon lemon juice

Drain strawberries, reserving syrup. Add enough orange juice to reserve syrup to make 1-1/2 cups. In a medium saucepan combine syrup mixture with sugar and cornstarch. Bring to a boil and stir one minute. Stir in lemon juice, orange segments and strawberries. Keep hot until ready to serve. To serve, spoon hot fruit mixture over pancake wedges. Makes 6 servings.

Crumpets

You will need 4 crumpet rings or clean 7-oz. flat cans with the top and bottom removed to bake these crumpets. Serve with butter and jam.

1/4 cup warm milk, 110F (45C)

1 tablespoon active dry yeast

1 teaspoon sugar

3/4 cup sourdough starter

1 egg

2 tablespoons butter or margarine, melted

3/4 cup all-purpose flour

1/2 teaspoon salt

Combine the milk, yeast and sugar. Let stand for 10 minutes until foamy. Stir in sourdough starter, egg, butter or margarine, flour and salt. Cover loosely and let set for 45 minutes. Grease a large skillet or griddle and heat over medium heat. To test for correct temperature, sprinkle with a few drops of water. If the water sizzles, the griddle is hot enough. Grease inside of baking rings. Place rings on prepared griddle. Spoon 3 tablespoons batter into each ring and cook until bubbles appear on the top, about 7 minutes. Run knife between crumpet and sides of ring to loosen. Remove rings. Turn crumpet over and cook about 2 minutes to brown other side. Repeat with remaining batter. Makes 8 crumpets.

Bagels

Bagels can be made in many flavors, just add 3/4 cup dried blueberries or cranberries, raisins or even shredded carrots to this basic recipe. You can also sprinkle tops of bagels with caraway, poppy or sesame seeds just before baking.

3/4 cup warm water, 110F (45C)

1 tablespoon active dry yeast

3 tablespoons sugar

3/4 cup sourdough starter

1 tablespoon salt

4 to 5 cups all-purpose flour or bread flour

2 quarts water

In a large mixing bowl combine the water, yeast, sugar and sourdough starter. Let stand for 10 minutes. Mix in salt and enough flour to make a soft dough. Turn dough onto a lightly floured smooth surface. Clean and grease the mixing bowl, set aside. Knead dough for about 10 minutes until smooth and elastic. Place in greased bowl, cover loosely, let rise for 30 minutes. Punch dough down. Divide into 12 equal portions. Roll each into a ball. Use your thumb to poke a hole in the center of each ball. Then form into doughnut shapes. Cover with a damp towel and let rise 20 minutes. Grease a large baking sheet. Preheat oven to 375F (190C). Bring 2 quarts of water to a boil in large pot. Reduce heat to let water simmer. Float as many bagels in the simmering water as will fit. Simmer for 7 minutes. Remove bagels and drain on paper towels. When all have been boiled, place on prepared baking sheet. Bake about 30 minutes until tops are golden brown. Makes 12 bagels.

Banana-Pecan Waffles

A great way to use up bananas that have softened and turned brown. If you have too many of these bananas they can be frozen with the peel on until needed.

2 eggs

1-1/2 cups milk

3/4 cup sourdough starter

2 teaspoons baking powder

1 ripe banana, mashed

1/2 teaspoon vanilla extract

2 tablespoons sugar

3 tablespoons oil

2 cups all-purpose flour

1/2 cup pecans, chopped

Preheat the waffle baker. In a medium mixing bowl whip the eggs and milk. Stir in the sourdough starter, baking powder, banana, vanilla, sugar and oil. Add flour and nuts, stir until well mixed. Pour batter, about 1/2 cup per waffle, into preheated waffle iron and bake until golden brown. Makes about 6 waffles.

Main Course Breads

Breads are usually thought of as an accompaniment to a meal. But these sourdough breads are so flavorful and attractive I like to let them be the star in a meal. Once you have had a Sourdough Pizza Dough, all the others may taste a little boring. I suggest making a double batch of the dough to bake and freeze for future use. Then you can quickly put together a fresh-from-the-oven pizza that will have just the ingredients everyone asks for. In my family we sometimes have four types of toppings on one pizza. I divide it in quarters and top each section with a different combination of ingredients.

Sourdough Crepes are really quick to make and so versatile even children can make them easily. Fill them with fresh berries and sprinkle with powdered sugar or let the children spread them with jam or stewed fruit. When rolled up they make a very special snack.

Italian Panini translates into sandwiches filled with what you have on hand. Or, stop at the delicatessen and have them slice a little ham, turkey and prosciutto, and thin slices of provolone cheese. Build your sandwich with these ingredients, sprinkle with vinegar and oil and you have a mouth-watering sandwich. Any sourdough recipe that appeals to you can be used. The classic shape is slightly flattened, round and sliced horizontally. When filled to your heart's content, slice it into wedges and serve.

Sourdough Crepes

My children like to fill crepes with strawberry jam for an after-school treat. Apricot jam and chopped peanuts are also great.

3 eggs

1 cup all-purpose flour

1/2 cup sourdough starter

1 cup milk

Butter, margarine or nonstick spray coating

In a bowl mix all ingredients until smooth. A food processor or electric mixer works very well. Heat a crepe pan or 8-inch nonstick skillet. Coat lightly with butter, margarine or nonstick spray coating. Dip crepe pan into batter or pour about 2 tablespoons of batter into the skillet. Cook just until golden brown on underside and dry on top. Stack crepes with pieces of plastic wrap between. If not used at time of preparation, crepes can be wrapped and stored in the refrigerator for up to 1 week or frozen. Makes about 8 crepes.

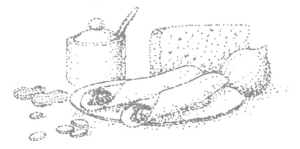

Olive-and-Ham Filling for Crepes

Use pitted ripe olives, green Spanish olives or pimento-stuffed olives if you prefer that flavor.

3 tablespoons butter or margarine

1/2 cup celery, finely sliced

1/2 medium onion, finely chopped

1/2 cup all-purpose flour

2 cups milk

2 oz. Gruyére cheese, shredded

1/4 teaspoon salt (optional)

1 teaspoon Dijon mustard

2 cups pitted olives, drained and chopped

1 cup ham, diced

8 Sourdough Crepes, page 92

Melt butter or margarine in a large skillet over medium heat. Sauté celery and onion until tender. Stir in flour. Cook and stir over medium heat for 1 minute. Gradually stir in milk, stirring until mixture is slightly thickened. Stir in cheese until melted. Add salt, mustard, olives and ham. Cook for 3 minutes longer to heat through. Place 1/2 cup of hot mixture along the center of each crepe and roll up. Place on serving platter. Garnish with additional whole olives if desired. If not serving immediately, reheat in the microwave or in a 350F (175C) oven for 15 minutes. Makes 8 crepes.

Cheese Blintzes

For your next brunch, serve these tender crepe packets of cheese with jam or fruit sauce.

1-1/2 cups cottage cheese

1 egg

1 tablespoon sugar

1 tablespoon vanilla extract

3 tablespoons butter or margarine

1 cup dairy sour cream

Strawberry or blueberry jam

12 Sourdough Crepes, page 92

Using a food processor or blender, combine the cottage cheese, egg, sugar and vanilla. Process until smooth. Spread about 2 tablespoons of this filling into the center of each crepe. Fold all sides of crepe over filling envelope-style. Melt butter or margarine 1 tablespoon at a time as needed in a large skillet over medium heat. Place filled crepes seam-side down in the skillet. Cook on both sides until golden brown and heated through. Serve topped with sour cream and jam. Makes 12 blintzes.

Make-Ahead Pizza Crust

Make a double batch and freeze it. For an extra-quick pizza, use bottled pizza sauce and add toppings, sliced vegetables, ham, ground meat, or Italian sausage.

1/4 cup warm water, 110F (45C)

2 teaspoons active dry yeast

1 teaspoon sugar

3 tablespoons vegetable oil

1 cup sourdough starter

3 to 3-1/2 cups bread flour

1 teaspoon salt

In a large mixing bowl combine the warm water, yeast and sugar. Stir and let stand for 10 minutes. Mix in oil, sourdough starter, one half the bread flour and the salt. Gradually add enough of the remaining bread flour to make a soft dough. Turn dough out onto a lightly floured smooth surface. Clean and grease the mixing bowl, set aside. Knead the dough for about 10 minutes until smooth and elastic. Place dough in greased bowl, turning to coat all sides. Cover and let rise until double in size, about 1 hour. Punch dough down and shape into two 12-inch flat rounds. Place on 12-inch ungreased pizza pans or baking sheets. Preheat oven to 400F (205C). Prebake 10 minutes but don't brown; set aside to cool. Wrap with plastic or foil and freeze or refrigerate until needed. When ready to use, top as desired and bake in a preheated 425F (220C) oven for 25 to 30 minutes. Makes 2 pizza crusts.

Island Pizza

Cut this pizza in small wedges for a tasty appetizer.

1 (12-inch) Make-Ahead Pizza Crust, page 95, room temperature

3 tablespoons prepared pesto sauce

1/4 lb. cooked, shelled bay shrimp

3/4 cup chopped marinated artichoke hearts

1/3 cup crushed pineapple, drained

1 cup (4 oz.) shredded Mozzarella cheese

Preheat oven to 425F (220C). Place pizza crust on ungreased baking sheet. Brush top of crust with pesto sauce. Sprinkle with shrimp, artichoke hearts and pineapple. Sprinkle with cheese. Bake in preheated oven for 10 to 12 minutes, until heated through. Makes one 12-inch pizza.

Mexican Pizza Olé

1 (12-inch) Make-Ahead Pizza Crust, page 95, room temperature

1 (16-oz.) can refried beans

1 cup salsa, drained

1/4 cup finely chopped cilantro

1 cup shredded cheddar cheese

1/2 cup thinly sliced green onions

Preheat oven to 425F (220C). Place pizza crust on ungreased baking sheet. Spread beans evenly on pizza crust. Spoon drained salsa on top. Sprinkle with cilantro, cheese and green onions. Bake in preheated oven for about 15 minutes until cheese is melted. Makes one 12-inch pizza.

Classic Pepperoni Pizza

Everyone seems to like pepperoni pizza. The sauce can be refrigerated for 5 days or frozen for future use.

**1 (12-inch) Make-Ahead Pizza Crust, page 95,
   room temperature**

Pizza sauce

4 ozs. pepperoni, thinly sliced

1 cup (4-oz.) shredded Mozzarella cheese

Preheat oven to 425F (220C). Prepare the pizza sauce. Spoon 1 cup sauce over pizza crust. Place the pepperoni evenly on top of sauce. Sprinkle with cheese. Place on an ungreased baking sheet and bake in preheated oven for 10 to 15 minutes until cheese is melted. Makes one 12-inch pizza.

Pizza Sauce

1/2 cup chopped green bell pepper

1/2 cup finely chopped onion

1 tablespoon olive oil

1 16-oz. can tomato sauce

1/4 teaspoon dried oregano

1/4 teaspoon Italian seasoning

To make Pizza Sauce:

In a medium skillet sauté the bell pepper and onion in the olive oil until tender. Mix in the tomato sauce, oregano and Italian seasoning. Cover and simmer for about 5 minutes. Makes 2 cups sauce.

Fresh-Tomato Pizza

Serve this as finger food rather than chips. Cut pizza in small wedges for a satisfying appetizer.

1 (12-inch) Make-Ahead Pizza Crust, page 95, room temperature

2 tablespoons olive oil

1/2 cup fresh basil leaves or 1 teaspoon dried basil

1 teaspoon finely chopped fresh oregano or 1/4 teaspoon dried

3 to 4 large tomatoes, sliced in 1/4-inch slices

3/4 cup goat cheese, crumbled

Preheat oven to 425F (220C). Place pizza crust on an ungreased baking sheet. Brush top of crust with olive oil. Sprinkle with basil and oregano. Arrange tomato slices on top of crust, overlapping slightly if necessary. Sprinkle with goat cheese. Bake in preheated oven for 10 to 12 minutes, until heated through. Makes one 12-inch pizza.

Mushroom and Onion Calzone

An Italian treat, filled with a flavorful combination of vegetables.

Dough

1/2 cup warm milk, 110F (45C)

1 teaspoon active dry yeast

1 cup sourdough starter

2 tablespoons olive oil

1/2 teaspoon salt

2-1/2 to 3 cups bread flour

In a large mixing bowl mix the milk and the yeast. Let stand for 10 minutes. Stir in the sourdough starter, olive oil, salt and one-half the flour. Add enough of the remaining flour to make a soft dough. Turn dough out onto a lightly floured smooth surface. Clean and grease the mixing bowl, set aside. Knead the dough for about 10 minutes until smooth and elastic. Place dough in greased bowl, turning to coat all sides. Cover and let rise until double in size, about 1 hour. Punch dough down and divide into 4 balls. Flatten each ball into a 9-inch round. Dough is now ready for the filling.

Mushroom and Onion Filling

2 cloves garlic, minced

2 tablespoons olive oil

1 large onion, thinly sliced

1/2 lb. mushrooms, thinly sliced

2 medium tomatoes, seeded and finely chopped

1/2 teaspoon dried marjoram

1 tablespoon fresh basil, finely chopped
    or 1 teaspoon dried

3 cups Swiss cheese, shredded

In a medium skillet, over medium heat, sauté the garlic in olive oil until translucent. Add the onions and cook until limp. Add the mushrooms, tomatoes, marjoram and basil. Stir to cook evenly until moisture is evaporated. Spoon mushroom mixture evenly onto the dough rounds. Sprinkle with cheese. Brush outside top edge of each bread round with water. Fold dough in half, leaving a 1/2-inch of bottom half showing. Fold that 1/2-inch up and over top dough. Crimp to seal well. Place on an ungreased baking sheet and cover loosely. Let rise for about 20 minutes. Preheat oven to 450F (230C). Bake Calzone for 12 to 15 minutes until golden brown. Makes 4 Calzones.

New England Clam Chowder Served in Bread Bowls

If fresh clams are available, use about 10 cherrystone clams. Steam them first, then clean. Chop clams coarsely and add to recipe. If soup is too thick add 1/2 cup milk to thin.

3/4 cup onion, finely chopped

1/4 cup celery, finely chopped

1/4 cup butter or margarine

1/4 cup all-purpose flour

3 cups clam juice

3/4 cup peeled and diced potato

1/4 teaspoon pepper

1 bay leaf

1/4 teaspoon dried thyme leaves

1 cup cream

1 (8-oz.) can chopped clams, undrained

6 Sourdough Bread Bowls, opposite

In a large saucepan sauté the onion and celery in the butter or margarine until tender. Stir in the flour, then the clam juice. Add the potato, pepper, bay leaf and thyme. Simmer for about 5 minutes until potato is cooked. Stir in the cream and clams. Bring to a boil. Remove from heat. Remove bay leaf and ladle into bread bowls. Makes 6 servings.

Sourdough Bread Bowls

Creamy or very chunky soups work best served in these bread bowls. My favorite part is being able to eat the flavor-soaked bread when the soup is finished.

**1 recipe Basic Sourdough Bread
   or Basic Sourdough Whole-Wheat Bread**

Prepare bread dough through the first rising. Punch dough down and divide into 6 even pieces. Shape each into a round ball. Place on a baking sheet leaving 2 inches between. Let rise for 45 minutes or until double in size. Preheat oven to 375F (190C). Bake in preheated oven for 20 minutes or until light golden brown. Remove from oven and let cool. To hollow out loaves for soup bowls, use a sharp paring knife and cut a circle in the top about 3/4-inch from the sides and about 3/4-inch up from the bottom. Gently pull out bread core in pieces until you have an area large enough to hold the soup. Bake soup bowls at 375F (190C) for about 10 minutes just to dry out interior. Ladle soup in and serve immediately. Makes 6 servings.

Panini

Panini is the Italian word for great sandwiches. Try adding grilled slices of eggplant, zucchini or bell peppers. For the bread try the Caraway, Anise and Sesame Seed Baguette dough baked into a 10-inch round.

1 (10-inch round) loaf of bread

1/2 cup bottled Italian salad dressing or your favorite vinaigrette

1/2 head curly leaf lettuce

1 lb. goat cheese, cut into 1/4-inch thick slices

1 cucumber, thinly sliced

12 slices tomatoes

1 small red onion, peeled and thinly sliced

1/2 cup chopped black olives

1/2 cup fresh basil leaves or a sprinkling of dried basil leaves

Freshly ground pepper

Cut bread in half horizontally, and scoop out some of the inside of the top half. Brush inside of both top and bottom with salad dressing. Arrange lettuce on bottom half and top with cheese. Layer cucumber and tomato slices. Spread onion slices over tomatoes. Sprinkle with olives and basil. Sprinkle with pepper. Place top on sandwich. Cut into wedges and serve. Makes 8 servings.

Brushetta

The Basic Sourdough Bread or the Pumpernickel work great as baguettes in this easy-to-fix appetizer recipe.

3 tablespoons olive oil

**1 tablespoon chopped fresh basil leaves
  or 1 teaspoon dried basil leaves**

1/2 teaspoon finely chopped fresh garlic

16 slices sourdough bread baguette, 1/2 inch thick

4 small ripe tomatoes, finely chopped

2 green onions, thinly sliced

1/4 cup (1-oz.) Mozzarella cheese, shredded

In a small bowl, stir together the olive oil, basil and garlic. Spread about 1 teaspoon olive-oil mixture on one side of each bread slice. Place bread slices on a baking sheet, then under the broiler 6 inches from heat. Broil until lightly toasted on each side for 1 to 2 minutes. Spoon tomatoes onto buttered side of each bread slice. Top each with about 1 teaspoon green onions and about 1-1/2 teaspoons cheese. Continue broiling until cheese is melted, 1 to 2 minutes. Makes 8 servings.

Oven-Baked French Toast

By baking French Toast in the oven you can cook enough for 6 servings at once. That way the cook can eat with everyone else.

12 slices bread

2 cups milk

6 eggs

2 tablespoons sugar

1/2 teaspoon ground cinnamon

Nonstick spray coating

Preheat oven to 450F (230C). Bread slices can be cut 1/2-inch to 3/4-inch thick. The thicker they are the longer they will need to cook. In a large pie plate whip together the milk, eggs, sugar and cinnamon. Spray two large jellyroll pans with the nonstick coating. Dip each slice of bread into egg mixture so all sides are coated. Place on prepared pan. Bake in preheated oven for 5 to 7 minutes, then turn bread slices over. Bake 5 to 7 minutes longer. Makes 6 servings.

Bread Machine Baking

Bread Machine Basics

This symbol identifies a recipe specifically created for bread machines. These recipes can also be used with traditional baking methods.

Bread Machine Basics

Bread machines are a welcome appliance in any kitchen. These machines are wonderful for the person who savors fresh baked bread and does not have enough time to bake in the traditional way. They also a boon to those who find it difficult to accomplish the hand kneading process. Timers allow you to prepare ingredients at night and awaken to that marvelous scent of baked bread. Enthusiasts say it's like having your own resident baker.

A bread machine is especially nice to take along when you vacation away from home or travel in a motor home, when markets are not nearby.

For those who do not own a bread machine and are interested in purchasing one, there are a few points to remember when you go shopping. Check into the mid-priced range of bread machines: many have the same or similar features. There may be no need for you to purchase a top-of-the-line model. It is important that you select a machine that can handle whole-wheat flour (not all machines do). The recipes in this book were developed using a variety of machines made by different manufacturers.

Always measure ingredients very carefully. To measure the flour, place it in a large mixing bowl and gently scoop the flour into the measuring cup. Then with a knife or other straight-edge tool, scrape off the top to make the flour perfectly level. Do not tap the measuring cup or press down on the flour because this will give you an incorrect measurement.

When you are making bread by hand, the measurements can be less precise. Bread machine recipes are written using *exact* amounts. The quality of the final product depends on the machine, not you.

Don't be afraid to check what is going on in the machine. The dough should be well mixed after a few minutes and not too dry or wet. It should be a smooth ball of dough.

If this is the first time you have made a recipe, check the dough after about 10 minutes to be sure it is well mixed.

You can add a tablespoon or two of water if the dough is too dry and not gathered into a ball. Or add a tablespoon or two of flour if the dough looks very wet or feels sticky.

The early part of the mixing process is the only time you need to lift the lid. Lifting the lid during the last hour of baking will let out the heat and the bread may not bake completely.

Basics for a Perfect Product

For a perfectly baked loaf, all ingredients must be at room temperature when placed into the baking pan of the machine. Add ingredients in the order suggested by the manufacturer of the machine you are using.

Do not let anything fall into the machine where the heating unit is, or it will burn. Clean up any spills *before* turning the machine on. To avoid spills, remove the baking pan to add the ingredients and carefully return it to the machine.

If you have a machine with a separate yeast dispenser, always use it. The mixing sequence of your machine is geared to that. If the bread is to be baked hours later, you do not want the yeast to mix with the liquid until the machine starts mixing.

When using whole-wheat or other coarse flours, check the dough as it begins to mix. If the mixing blade seems to be stuck or straining, reach in with your hand and pick up the dough to free the blade. Tear off chunks of dough, place one at a time back into the machine. If the dough does not mix smoothly, add a tablespoon of water. Next time reverse the order in which the liquid and flour are added.

Let bread cool in the pan for 10 minutes before removing. Place baked bread on a rack to cook to room temperature before slicing. Hot bread tends to squash when sliced and is not very attractive.

Be sure to check the bottom of the loaf to be sure the kneading blade is not stuck in the bread.

Turn cooled bread on its side. Slice with a serrated or electric knife using a sawing motion.

Because it has no preservatives, home-baked bread tends to dry out very quickly. To keep it fresh, wrap it in plastic as soon as it has cooled to room temperature.

Bread can be frozen as a whole loaf or sliced. Be sure it is wrapped tightly to prevent spoilage or freezer-drying from exposure to air.

Classic Sourdough Bread

This recipe uses no additional yeast. It relies completely on the sourdough sponge for raising the dough. It makes a dense but tasty loaf.

1 Pound Loaf	Ingredients	1-1/2 Pound Loaf
1 cup	Sourdough starter	1-1/2 cups
2-1/2 cups	Bread flour	3-3/4 cups
1/2 cup	Water	3/4 cup
1 tablespoon	Sugar	1-1/2 tablespoons
1 teaspoon	Salt	1-1/2 teaspoons

In a medium glass mixing bowl combine 1 cup (1-1/2 cups) starter, 1 cup (1-1/2 cups) bread flour and 1/2 cup (3/4 cup) water. Mix well, cover and set aside for 8 hours or overnight. It should be full of bubbles. To mix bread, place starter and remaining ingredients in machine. Select the MEDIUM setting and start the machine. The finished loaf will be dense and very flavorful.

*Ingredients listed in parenthesis are for the 1-1/2 pound loaf.

Basic Sourdough Bread

Don't forget to replenish your starter after each loaf you bake. This tasty bread gets eaten up quickly and you'll want to bake more.

1 Pound Loaf	Ingredients	1-1/2 Pound Loaf
1 cup	Sourdough starter	1-1/2 cups
1/4 cup	Milk	1/3 cup
2 tablespoons	Butter or margarine	3 tablespoons
2 cups	Bread flour	3 cups
1 tablespoon	Sugar	1-1/2 tablespoons
3/4 teaspoon	Salt	1 teaspoon
1 teaspoon	Active dry yeast	1 teaspoon

Add ingredients to the machine in the order suggested by the manufacturer. Use the LIGHT setting. Let bread cool in the pan for 10 minutes before removing. Place loaf on a rack to cool completely.

Basic Sour Rye

The caraway seeds can be increased if you really love the taste.
If not omit them entirely or substitute sesame seeds.

1 Pound Loaf	Ingredients	1-1/2 Pound Loaf
1 cup	**Sourdough starter**	1-1/2 cups
1/4 cup	**Water**	1/3 cup
1 tablespoon	**Butter or margarine**	1-1/2 tablespoons
1 cup	**Bread flour**	1-1/2 cups
1-1/4 cups	**Rye flour**	1-3/4 cups
1 tablespoon	**Caraway seeds**	1-1/2 tablespoons
1 tablespoon	**Sugar**	1-1/2 tablespoons
1 teaspoon	**Salt**	1-1/4 teaspoons
1 teaspoon	**Active dry yeast**	1-1/2 teaspoons

Add ingredients to the machine in the order suggested by
the manufacturer. Use the MEDIUM setting. Let bread cool in
the pan for 10 minutes before removing. Place loaf on a
rack to cool completely.

Basic Sourdough Whole-Wheat Loaf

Honey and whole-wheat flavors add a special taste to this wholesome bread.

1 Pound Loaf	Ingredients	1-1/2 Pound Loaf
3/4 cup	Sourdough starter	1-1/3 cups
3 tablespoons	Milk	1/4 cup
2 tablespoons	Butter or margarine	3 tablespoons
1 cup	Bread flour	1-1/2 cups
1 cup	Whole-wheat flour	1-1/2 cups
2 tablespoons	Honey	3 tablespoons
1 teaspoon	Salt	1-1/2 teaspoons
1 teaspoon	Active dry yeast	1 teaspoon

Add ingredients to the machine in the order suggested by the manufacturer. Use the MEDIUM setting. Let bread cool in the pan for 10 minutes before removing. Place loaf on a rack to cool completely.

Basic Egg Bread

The addition of an egg or two tends to make the loaves just a little bit lighter in texture, and brighter in color.

1 Pound Loaf	Ingredients	1-1/2 Pound Loaf
3/4 cup	Sourdough starter	1 cup
1/3 cup	Milk	3/4 cup
1 tablespoon	Oil	1-1/2 tablespoons
1	Egg	2
2 cups	Bread flour	3 cups
1 teaspoon	Sugar	1-1/2 teaspoons
3/4 teaspoon	Salt	1 teaspoon
1 teaspoon	Active dry yeast	1 teaspoon

Add ingredients to the machine in the order suggested by the manufacturer. Use the LIGHT setting. Let bread cool in the pan for 10 minutes before removing. Place loaf on a rack to cool completely.

Orange-Marmalade Rye Bread

I always liked the flavor of marmalade on rye toast. With this recipe you just toast a slice and butter.

1 Pound Loaf	Ingredients	1-1/2 Pound Loaf
1/2 cup	Sourdough starter	3/4 cup
1 tablespoon	Butter or margarine	1-1/2 tablespoons
2 tablespoons	Water	3 tablespoons
1-1/4 cups	Bread flour	2 cups
1 cup	Rye flour	1-1/3 cups
1/2 cup	Orange marmalade	3/4 cup
1 tablespoon	Sugar	1-1/2 tablespoons
1/2 teaspoon	Salt	3/4 teaspoon
1 tablespoon	Active dry yeast	1-1/2 tablespoons

Add ingredients to the machine in the order suggested by the manufacturer. Use the LIGHT setting. Let bread cool in the pan for 10 minutes before removing. Place loaf on a rack to cool completely.

Pineapple-Pecan Whole-Wheat

Be sure to drain the pineapple well. If you like a more pronounced fruit flavor, use the drained pineapple juice. Add enough water if necessary to equal the correct measurement.

1 Pound Loaf	Ingredients	1-1/2 Pound Loaf
1/2 cup	Sourdough starter	3/4 cup
1/4 cup	Water and/or drained pineapple juice	1/2 cup
1 tablespoon	Butter or margarine	1-1/2 tablespoons
1 cup	Bread flour	1-1/2 cups
1 cup	Whole-wheat flour	1-1/2 cups
1/2 cup	Canned, crushed pineapple, drained	3/4 cup
1/2 cup	Pecans, coarsely chopped and toasted	3/4 cup
1/2 teaspoon	Salt	3/4 teaspoon
1 teaspoon	Active dry yeast	1 teaspoon

Add ingredients to the machine in the order suggested by the manufacturer. Use the MEDIUM setting. Let bread cool in the pan for 10 minutes before removing. Place loaf on a rack to cool completely.

Whole-Wheat Fruit Bread

*Packages of the assorted dried fruit can be found in the
grocery store, usually right next to the raisins.*

1 Pound Loaf	Ingredients	1-1/2 Pound Loaf
1/2 cup	Sourdough starter	3/4 cup
1/2 cup	Orange juice	3/4 cup
1 tablespoon	Butter or margarine	1-1/2 tablespoons
1 cup	Bread flour	1-1/2 cups
1 cup	Whole-wheat flour	1-1/2 cups
3/4 cup	Assorted dried fruit finely chopped	1-1/4 cups
3/4 teaspoon	Ground nutmeg	1 teaspoon
1 tablespoon	Sugar	1-1/2 tablespoons
1/2 teaspoon	Salt	3/4 teaspoon
1 teaspoon	Active dry yeast	1 teaspoon

Add ingredients to the machine in the order suggested by
the manufacturer. Use the LIGHT setting. Let bread cool in
the pan for 10 minutes before removing. Place loaf on a
rack to cool completely.

Cranberry Pecan Whole-Wheat Bread

Try substituting dried blueberries or cherries for the cranberries.

1 Pound Loaf	Ingredients	1-1/2 Pound Loaf
3/4 cup	Sourdough starter	1 cup
1/2 cup	Water	3/4 cup
1 cup	Bread flour	1-1/2 cups
1 cup	Whole-wheat flour	1-1/2 cups
3/4 cup	Dried cranberries	1 cup
1/3 cup	Pecans, whole	1/2 cup
1 tablespoon	Sugar	1-1/2 tablespoons
3/4 teaspoon	Salt	1 teaspoon
1 teaspoon	Active dry yeast	1 teaspoon

Add ingredients to the machine in the order suggested by the manufacturer. Use the LIGHT setting. Let bread cool in the pan for 10 minutes before removing. Place loaf on a rack to cool completely.

Cinnamon-Apple Bread

This bread has the same tantalizing aroma as a fresh apple pie.
Serve it with thin slices of Cheddar cheese.

1 Pound Loaf	Ingredients	1-1/2 Pound Loaf
1/2 cup	Sourdough starter	3/4 cup
1/4 cup	Milk	1/3 cup
1 tablespoon	Butter or margarine	2 tablespoons
2-1/4 cups	Bread flour	3-1/3 cups
1/4 teaspoon	Ground nutmeg	1/2 teaspoon
1 teaspoon	Ground cinnamon	1-1/2 teaspoons
1 cup	Apple, peeled and finely chopped	1-1/2 cups
2 tablespoons	Brown sugar	3 tablespoons
1/2 teaspoon	Salt	3/4 teaspoon
1 teaspoon	Active dry yeast	1 teaspoon

Add ingredients to the machine in the order suggested by
the manufacturer. Use the LIGHT setting. Let bread cool in
the pan for 10 minutes before removing. Place loaf on a
rack to cool completely.

Whole-Wheat Raisin-Walnut Loaf

For an easy sandwich spread thin slices of this bread with
cream cheese.

1 Pound Loaf	Ingredients	1-1/2 Pound Loaf
1/2 cup	Sourdough starter	3/4 cup
1/2 cup	Milk	3/4 cup
1 tablespoon	Oil	1-1/2 tablespoons
1/2 cup	Bread flour	3/4 cup
1-1/2 cups	Whole-wheat flour	2-1/4 cups
1 teaspoon	Ground cinnamon (optional)	1-1/2 teaspoons
3/4 cup	Light raisins	1 cup
1/2 cup	Walnuts, finely chopped	3/4 cup
1 teaspoon	Sugar	1-1/2 teaspoons
1/2 teaspoon	Salt	3/4 teaspoon
1 teaspoon	Active dry yeast	1 teaspoon

Add ingredients to the machine in the order suggested by
the manufacturer. Use the MEDIUM setting. Let bread cool
in the pan for 10 minutes before removing. Place loaf on a
rack to cool completely.

Blueberry-Nut Loaf

If you can't find dried blueberries in your market, try a specialty food store. You could easily substitute dried cranberries, apricots or dates for the blueberries.

1 Pound Loaf	Ingredients	1-1/2 Pound Loaf
1/2 cup	Sourdough starter	3/4 cup
1/3 cup	Orange juice	3/4 cup
1 tablespoon	Butter or margarine	1-1/2 tablespoons
2 cups	Bread flour	3 cups
3/4 cup	Dried blueberries	1 cup
1 tablespoon	Grated orange peel	1-1/2 tablespoons
1/3 cup	Pecans, chopped coarsely	1/2 cup
2 tablespoons	Sugar	3 tablespoons
1/2 teaspoon	Salt	3/4 teaspoon
1 teaspoon	Active dry yeast	1 teaspoon

Add ingredients to the machine in the order suggested by the manufacturer. Use the LIGHT setting. Let bread cool in the pan for 10 minutes before removing. Place loaf on a rack to cool completely.

Banana-Nut Bread

Banana bread is usually made as a quick bread, but try this method to use up extra bananas. It's great for peanut-butter-and-jelly sandwiches that people of all ages will enjoy.

1 Pound Loaf	Ingredients	1-1/2 Pound Loaf
1/2 cup	Sourdough starter	3/4 cup
2 tablespoons	Milk	1/4 cup
1	Egg	1
1 tablespoon	Oil	2 tablespoons
1/3 cup	Ripe banana, mashed	1/2 cup
1-1/2 cups	Bread flour	2-1/4 cups
3/4 cup	Whole-wheat flour	1 cup
1/4 cup	Chopped walnuts	1/2 cup
1 tablespoon	Sugar	2 tablespoons
1/4 teaspoon	Salt	1/2 teaspoon
2 teaspoons	Active dry yeast	2 teaspoons

Add ingredients to the machine in the order suggested by the manufacturer. Use the LIGHT setting. Let bread cool in the pan for 10 minutes before removing. Place loaf on a rack to cool completely.

Cottage-Cheese Chive Loaf

Substitute equal amounts of dried currants for the chives to give this bread an entirely different, but equally tasty flavor.

1 Pound Loaf	Ingredients	1-1/2 Pound Loaf
1/2 cup	Sourdough starter	3/4 cup
1/2 cup	Cottage cheese	3/4 cup
1 cup	Bread flour	1-1/2 cups
1 cup	Whole-wheat flour	1-1/2 cups
1/4 cup	Chives, finely chopped	1/3 cup
1 tablespoon	Sugar	1-1/2 tablespoons
1 teaspoon	Salt	1-1/2 teaspoons
1 teaspoon	Active dry yeast	1 teaspoon

Add ingredients to the machine in the order suggested by the manufacturer. Use the MEDIUM setting. Let bread cool in the pan for 10 minutes before removing. Place loaf on a rack to cool completely.

Tomato-Feta Loaf

Feta cheese has a wonderful salty flavor and adds a light texture to this bread.

1 Pound Loaf	Ingredients	1-1/2 Pound Loaf
1/2 cup	Sourdough starter	3/4 cup
1/3 cup	Water	3/4 cup
2 cups	Bread flour	3 cups
1/3 cup	Feta cheese, crumbled	1/2 cup
1/4 cup	Green onion stems, finely chopped	1/2 cup
1/2 cup	Sun-dried tomatoes in oil, drained, finely chopped	3/4 cup
1 teaspoon	Sugar	1 teaspoon
1/4 teaspoon	Salt	1/2 teaspoon
1 teaspoon	Active dry yeast	1 teaspoon

Add ingredients to the machine in the order suggested by the manufacturer. Use the MEDIUM setting. Let bread cool in the pan for 10 minutes before removing. Place loaf on a rack to cool completely.

Pesto Bread

Classic pesto is made from fresh basil, Parmesan cheese and olive oil, this bread has all the same ingredients. Serve with a saucer of olive oil to dip it in.

1 Pound Loaf	Ingredients	1-1/2 Pound Loaf
3/4 cup	Sourdough starter	1-1/4 cups
1/3 cup	Milk	1/2 cup
2 tablespoons	Olive oil	3 tablespoons
2 cups	Bread flour	3 cups
1/4 cup	Pine nuts, toasted	1/3 cup
1/4 cup	Fresh basil leaves, finely chopped	1/3 cup
1/3 cup	Grated Parmesan cheese	1/2 cup
1/2 teaspoon	Sugar	3/4 teaspoon
3/4 teaspoon	Salt	1 teaspoon
1 teaspoon	Active dry yeast	1 teaspoon

Add ingredients to the machine in the order suggested by the manufacturer. Use the LIGHT setting. Let bread cool in the pan for 10 minutes before removing. Place loaf on a rack to cool completely.

Chili-Cheese Corn Bread

To serve this bread cut it in 1-1/2-inch-thick slices, then cut each slice into quarters, serve warm

1 Pound Loaf	Ingredients	1-1/2 Pound Loaf
1/2 cup	Sourdough starter	3/4 cup
1/4 cup	Water	1/2 cup
2 tablespoons	Oil	3 tablespoons
1-3/4 cups	Bread flour	2-3/4 cups
1/2 cup	Cornmeal	3/4 cup
2 tablespoons	Chopped black olives	3 tablespoons
1/4 cup	Canned diced Anaheim chilies	1/3 cup
1/2 cup	Shredded Cheddar cheese	3/4 cup
1/2 cup	Frozen whole-kernel corn	3/4 cup
1 tablespoon	Sugar	1-1/2 tablespoons
1-1/2 teaspoons	Salt	2 teaspoons
1-1/2 teaspoons	Active dry yeast	2 teaspoons

Add ingredients to the machine in the order suggested by the manufacturer. Use the MEDIUM setting. Let bread cool in the pan for 10 minutes before removing. Place loaf on a rack to cool completely.

Pumpkin Bread

All the flavor and aroma of pumpkin pie. Try a slice of this toasted and spread with cream cheese or whipped honey.

1 Pound Loaf	Ingredients	1-1/2 Pound Loaf
1/2 cup	Sourdough starter	3/4 cup
1/4 cup	Water	1/3 cup
1 tablespoon	Butter or margarine	1-1/2 tablespoons
2-1/4 cups	Bread flour	3-1/2 cups
3/4 cup	Canned pumpkin	1 cup
1 teaspoon	Ground cinnamon	1-1/2 teaspoons
1/4 teaspoon	Ground nutmeg	1/2 teaspoon
2 tablespoons	Sugar	3 tablespoons
1/2 teaspoon	Salt	3/4 teaspoon
1 teaspoon	Active dry yeast	1 teaspoon

Add ingredients to the machine in the order suggested by the manufacturer. Use the LIGHT setting. Let bread cool in the pan for 10 minutes before removing. Place loaf on a rack to cool completely.

Green-Onion Basil Bread

Brush toasted slices of this bread with olive oil and top with thin slices of tomato and Swiss or Fontina cheese for a yummy appetizer.

1 Pound Loaf	Ingredients	1-1/2 Pound Loaf
1/2 cup	Sourdough starter	3/4 cup
1/3 cup	Water	3/4 cup
1 tablespoon	Olive oil	2 tablespoons
2 cups	Bread flour	3 cups
1/4 cup	Green onion, chopped	1/3 cup
1/4 cup	Fresh basil leaves, chopped or	1/3 cup
1 tablespoon	Dried basil leaves	1-1/2 tablespoons
1 clove	Garlic, minced	1 to 2 cloves
1 teaspoon	Sugar	2 teaspoons
1/2 teaspoon	Salt	3/4 teaspoon
1 teaspoon	Active dry yeast	1 teaspoon

Add ingredients to the machine in the order suggested by the manufacturer. Use the LIGHT setting. Let bread cool in the pan for 10 minutes before removing. Place loaf on a rack to cool completely.

Bell-Pepper Olive Bread

Bell peppers come in so many colors that you can use red, green, yellow, orange or any combination to make it look like confetti.

1 Pound Loaf	Ingredients	1-1/2 Pound Loaf
1 cup	Sourdough starter	1-1/2 cups
1/4 cup	Milk	1/3 cup
1 tablespoon	Vegetable oil	1-1/2 tablespoons
1-1/4 cups	Bread flour	1-3/4 cups
1 cup	Whole-wheat flour	1-1/2 cups
1/2 cup	Bell pepper, finely chopped	3/4 cup
1/2 cup	Green olives, pitted and finely chopped	3/4 cup
1 teaspoon	Sugar	1-1/2 teaspoons
1/2 teaspoon	Salt	3/4 teaspoon
2 teaspoons	Active dry yeast	2 teaspoons

Add ingredients to the machine in the order suggested by the manufacturer. Use the LIGHT setting. Let bread cool in the pan for 10 minutes before removing. Place loaf on a rack to cool completely.

Raisin-Rosemary Bread

*Fresh rosemary is a very important ingredient in this recipe.
I don't recommend substituting dried rosemary.*

1 Pound Loaf	Ingredients	1-1/2 Pound Loaf
3/4 cup	Sourdough starter	1 cup
1/4 cup	Milk	1/3 cup
2 tablespoons	Butter or margarine	3 tablespoons
2 cups	Bread flour	3 cups
2 tablespoons	Coarsely chopped fresh rosemary leaves	3 tablespoons
1/2 cup	Raisins	2/3 cup
1 tablespoon	Sugar	1-1/2 tablespoons
1 teaspoon	Salt	1-1/2 teaspoons
1 teaspoon	Active dry yeast	1 teaspoon

Add ingredients to the machine in the order suggested by
the manufacturer. Use the MEDIUM setting. Let bread cool in
the pan for 10 minutes before removing. Place loaf on a
rack to cool completely.

Carrot-Tarragon Loaf

Try adding a pinch of tarragon to steamed carrots the next time you have them for dinner. It's an intriguing taste combination.

1 Pound Loaf	Ingredients	1-1/2 Pound Loaf
1/2 cup	Sourdough starter	3/4 cup
1/3 cup	Milk	3/4 cup
1 tablespoon	Butter or margarine	2 tablespoons
2 cups	Bread flour	3 cups
3/4 cup	Grated carrots	1-1/4 cups
3/4 tablespoon	Finely chopped fresh tarragon leaves	1 tablespoon
	or	
1 teaspoon	Dried tarragon, leaves, crushed	1-1/4 teaspoons
1 teaspoon	Sugar	1 teaspoon
1 teaspoon	Salt	1-1/4 teaspoons
1 teaspoon	Active dry yeast	1 teaspoon

Add ingredients to the machine in the order suggested by the manufacturer. Use the LIGHT setting. Let bread cool in the pan for 10 minutes before removing. Place loaf on a rack to cool completely.

Anadama Bread

The combination of molasses and cornmeal in this bread are a good clue to its New England heritage.

1 Pound Loaf	Ingredients	1-1/2 Pound Loaf
1/2 cup	Sourdough starter	3/4 cup
1/4 cup	Milk	1/2 cup
1 tablespoon	Butter or margarine	2 tablespoons
1-1/2 cups	Bread flour	2-1/4 cups
1/2 cup	Cornmeal	3/4 cup
1/2 cup	Rye flour	3/4 cup
1/4 cup	Molasses	1/3 cup
1/2 teaspoon	Salt	3/4 teaspoon
1 teaspoon	Active dry yeast	2 teaspoons

Add ingredients to the machine in the order suggested by the manufacturer. Use the LIGHT setting. Let bread cool in the pan for 10 minutes before removing. Place loaf on a rack to cool completely.

Multi-Grain Bread

Start off your morning with this healthy delicious bread.
It makes great toast.

1 Pound Loaf	Ingredients	1-1/2 Pound Loaf
1 cup	Sourdough starter	1-1/2 cups
2 tablespoons	Water	1/4 cup
2 tablespoons	Olive oil	3 tablespoons
1 cup	Bread flour	1-1/2 cups
1/2 cup	Whole-wheat flour	3/4 cup
1/2 cup	Rye flour	3/4 cup
2 tablespoons	Sunflower seeds	3 tablespoons
1 tablespoon	Wheat germ	1-1//2 tablespoons
2 tablespoons	Rolled oats	3 tablespoons
1 tablespoon	Honey	2 tablespoons
1/2 teaspoon	Salt	3/4 teaspoon
2 teaspoons	Active dry yeast	2 teaspoons

Add ingredients to the machine in the order suggested by the manufacturer. Use the LIGHT setting. Let bread cool in the pan for 10 minutes before removing. Place loaf on a rack to cool completely.

Sunflower-Seed Bread

If the sunflower seeds are salted, put them in a strainer and rinse. Shake off any excess water before placing them in the bread machine.

1 Pound Loaf	Ingredients	1-1/2 Pound Loaf
1/2 cup	**Sourdough starter**	3/4 cup
1/4 cup	**Milk**	3/4 cup
1 tablespoon	**Oil**	2 tablespoons
2/3 cup	**Bread flour**	1 cup
1-1/4 cups	**Whole-wheat flour**	2 cups
2 tablespoons	**Sunflower seeds**	3 tablespoons
1 tablespoon	**Honey**	2 tablespoons
1/2 teaspoon	**Salt**	3/4 teaspoon
1 teaspoon	**Active dry yeast**	1 teaspoon

Add ingredients to the machine in the order suggested by the manufacturer. Use the MEDIUM setting. Let bread cool in the pan for 10 minutes before removing. Place loaf on a rack to cool completely.

Brioche-Type Sandwich Bread

When using a large quantity of butter or margarine, be sure to cut it into 1/2-inch chunks before adding to the mixture so it will blend into the dough more evenly.

1 Pound Loaf	Ingredients	1-1/2 Pound Loaf
1/3 cup	Sourdough starter	1/2 cup
2	Eggs	3
1/3 cup	Butter or margarine, room temperature	1/2 cup
2 cups	Bread Flour	3 cups
1 teaspoon	Sugar	1-1/2 teaspoons
1/2 teaspoon	Salt	3/4 teaspoon
2 teaspoons	Active dry yeast	2 teaspoons

Add ingredients to the machine in the order suggested by the manufacturer. Use the LIGHT setting. Let bread cool in the pan for 10 minutes before removing. Place loaf on a rack to cool completely.

Index

137